More praise for *Translating from the Portuguese: A Life Translated*

With these revelatory vignettes, Elizabeth Lowe, one our most cherished literary translators of Brazilian and Portuguese literatures, offers readers a glimpse into her life and work. Lowe moves beyond memoir to include compelling chronicles of translating some of the greatest literary voices from the region (Machado de Assis, Lispector, and João de Melo, among others) and thoughtful reflections on topics that most concern translators today. At a moment when literary translation has become quite fashionable, *Translating from the Portuguese* is an essential volume that gives voice to an innovator who helped pave the way to our present moment.

Katherine M. Hedeen is a Professor of Spanish at Kenyon College and Managing Editor of Action Books.

The third section is a particular delight for readers like me who have some familiarity with its subjects, as it looks at about a dozen writers Lowe has translated (with a chronological range from Machado de Assis to JP Cuenca, and from the very widely known – Clarice Lispector, say – to the less familiar, such as Victor Giudice). For most of those working in the last half-century there are personal encounters – often enduring friendships – in addition to descriptions of their work, suggestions of the challenges they pose to a translator. As a translator who has lived in each of these writers' work so intensely, Lowe is able to fill the whole section with fascinating insights.

Daniel Hahn is a British writer, editor, and translator. He serves on the board of trustees of the Society of Authors, and several other organizations working with literature, literacy, and free expression, including English PEN, The Children's Bookshow, and Modern Poetry in Translation. His book on translation, *Catching Fire: a Translation Diary*, was published in 2022.

In her eloquently written memoir, *Translating from the Portuguese: A Life in Translation*, Elizabeth Lowe explores the intricate and far-reaching relationships between travel and translation and how they have helped forge her own identity and career. Lowe draws upon a plethora of influences and achievements: her German-Jewish family background; her linguistic and cultural immersion in countries including post-WWII Germany, and Haiti, Colombia, and Brazil during moments of political upheaval; her studies at the CUNY Graduate Center with the great Gregory Rabassa; her vast experience translating works of Latin American literature—most notably by iconic Brazilian authors Clarice Lispector, Rubem Fonseca, and Nélida Piñon—and as an author of literary criticism; as well as her role as founder of groundbreaking translation programs at major U.S. universities. Her astute weaving together of these diverse strands, including a whole section devoted to translation principles and their application that underscores the primacy of the word and translation as creative writing, culminates in a rich portrait of her formation as a world citizen, an active practitioner of the art of translation, and a role model for current and future translators, writers, and scholars. Elizabeth Lowe's memoir is an essential resource for aspiring translators, not to mention an exciting read for travelers and lovers of literature. To paraphrase the epigraph by Emily Dickinson that introduces the book and is referenced at its conclusion, it's a veritable touchstone for all those who "dwell in possibility."

Daniel Shapiro is Editor of *Review: Literature and Arts of the Americas.*

Translating from the Portuguese
A Life Translated

Translating from the Portuguese
A Life Translated

Elizabeth Lowe

Tagus Press. University of Massachusetts Dartmouth. Dartmouth, MA

Tagus Press is the publishing arm of the Center for Portuguese Studies and Culture at the University of Massachusetts Dartmouth.
Center director: Anna M. Klobucka

Tagus Press at the University of Massachusetts Dartmouth

Manufactured in the United States of America
Executive Editor: Mario Pereira

Copyedited by Laura Reed-Morrisson
Designed and typeset by: Inês Sena
Cover illustration: Constança Penedo

For all inquiries, please contact:
Tagus Press, Center for Portuguese Studies and Culture
University of Massachusetts Dartmouth
285 Old Westport Road, North Dartmouth, MA 02747–2300
(508) 999-8255, fax (508) 999-9272
https://www.umassd.edu/portuguese-studies-center/
ISBN: 978-1-951470-34-0
Library of Congress control number: 2025933333

Grateful acknowledgement is made to Elisabeth Hallett for permission to reproduce "Rio" from *Still Mystified: The Poems in My Life*. Copyright 2003 by Elisabeth Hallett. Grateful acknowledgement is made to Katherine M. Hedeen for permission to reproduce "Manifesto?" from *Asymptote*. Copyright 2019 by Katherine M. Hedeen.

For my granddaughters,
Sarah Anne Misarti
and Amanda Charlotte Misarti

I dwell in Possibility –
A fairer House than Prose –
More numerous of Windows –
Superior – for Doors –

Of Chambers as the Cedars –
Impregnable of eye –
And for an everlasting Roof
The Gambrels of the Sky –

Of Visitors – the fairest –
For Occupation – This –
The spreading wide my narrow Hands
To gather Paradise –

Emily Dickinson

We translate to be translated.

Suzanne Jill Levine, The Subversive Scribe

I lost two cities, lovely ones. And, vaster,
some realms I owned, two rivers, a continent.
I miss them, but it wasn't a disaster.

Elizabeth Bishop, "One Art"

A book is not an isolated being, it is a relationship, an axis of innumerable relationships.

Jorge Luis Borges, "A Note on (toward) Bernard Shaw"

Contents

Author's Note

This is not a traditional memoir, but rather a series of vignettes and reflections on my life in translation, on teaching translation, and on the art and craft of translation. Growing up as an expatriate shaped my life and worldview, leading me to live in and through several languages—and to work and dream in those languages. Truly, as Charlemagne once reputedly said, "To have a second language is to possess a second soul." By that count, I have at least five. The expatriate life drew me naturally into the professional world of translation, both as a practitioner of literary translation and as a scholar and teacher. The historical and political moments of the countries I lived in framed my experiences by demanding constant negotiation between languages and circumstances: Nuremberg immediately after the war and the trials, Haiti just prior to Papa Doc's consolidation of power, Brazil during the dictatorship, Portugal during the Salazar period, Germany during the Vietnam War, and Colombia during the height of the guerrilla conflicts gave me a sense of the immediacy and relevance of context to the linguistic and cultural experience. This is why I reference those historical moments in my vignettes: they had a deep impact on my understanding of place. Taking a cue from Kate Briggs in *This Little Art*, I chart my journey in a nonlinear way, with the intention of illustrating how each life event has contributed to my formation. Suzanne Jill Levine, whom I have known since our college days in the late 1960s, wrote in her book *The Subversive Scribe* that we "translate to be translated" (2009, v). My work with individual Portuguese-language authors is chronicled in the book; these relationships were fundamental to my development as a writer and as a human being. While I have translated many texts from the Spanish, the literature by the Lusophone writers with whom I have spent most of my time represents the core of my work and has, in every sense, motivated me to translate and, in so doing, "to be translated."

Introduction

March 20, 2022

Spring will arrive in Dartmouth, Massachusetts, at 11:33 am today. I have spent the winter here as a visiting professor at University of Massachusetts Dartmouth, snugly housed in Thistle Cottage, a mile away from campus. In the sunroom that has become my study, I have observed the gelid world around me in its dormant, dazzling mystery. I lived most of my life in the Caribbean, Central and South America, and Florida, apart from winters in my home city, New York, or in Champaign-Urbana, Illinois, Munich, and Vienna. This return to cold weather, and to the heart of the Portuguese diaspora in the United States in the adjoining communities of New Bedford, Dartmouth, and Fall River, has been a time of renewal and reflection. It has brought me full circle to the area of study and teaching where I began my journey in the literature of the Portuguese-speaking world. It has helped me redefine myself, connect deeply to my students, and decide that my next important task is to write about what I have experienced and learned in a life in translation. My growing-up years in a multitude of cultural and linguistic environments formed me and laid the foundation for my life's work. This might be a helpful guide to those wishing to embark on the translation path as well as an affirmation that learning languages as a child (or at any time in life) is what we as humans are equipped to do and that the gift of multilingualism and multiculturalism pays many dividends, personally and collectively. I believe that translation, as the finest act of communication, is also an act of self-discovery and self-affirmation. By inhabiting two or more languages and cultures, translators are trained to cultivate the arts of listening, reading, and writing. We also learn to assess who we are and to honor ourselves as multicultural, multilingual, and multinational beings. We go through life in a state of *Fernweh*, the pain of longing to travel far, which is paired with *Reiselust*, or wanderlust, which is the utter joy of travel. This leads to the need to experience what is beyond our doorstep; not fully belonging anywhere, and belonging everywhere, we make ourselves at home in any setting. A related concept is *weltfremd*, which can mean "like a stranger in the world," "out of touch with reality," "alienated," or even "idealistic," in a quixotic sense. We are chameleons who shape-shift our speech, fine-tune our hearing, sharpen our sense of smell and touch, and train our eyes to blend in with the place where we are. We expend our energy observing and learning about our surroundings. The texts that we choose to translate, and rewrite, are a complement to this way of exploring the world. Our mission as translators is to bring important books to new audiences who cannot read them in the original language. What writers in other countries have to say is relevant to understanding our own world; the shared experience of the other creates a human bond that transcends borders and can heal common wounds. Translation done well can be an act of peacemaking. It is also an act of becoming. In Jhumpa Lahiri's words, "To be a writer-translator is to value both being and becoming. What one writes in any given language typically remains as is, but translation pushes it to become otherwise" (2023, 8).

This morning, swans are gliding in the pond across from my window, the forsythia is budding, and crocus and daffodils are valiantly pushing their tiny blossoms out of the thawing soil. A warm wind is blowing in from Buzzard's Bay; the days are lengthening. The calls of red-winged blackbirds and peepers announce the change of season. As I move into another season of my life, one that some would call winter but I think of as another spring in my life trajectory, I write this book to honor my teachers and those brilliant translators who paved the way for me. It is also for all who come after me, with the expectation that they will enlarge the world and make it a safer and better place with their work in languages, cultures, and translation. My wish for future translators and translation scholars is that they will discover that their relationship with the texts and authors they translate brings them a bigger life, richer in possibilities.

Thistle Cottage

The thistle, a national emblem of Scotland and the base of Scotland's ancient order of chivalry known as The Order of the Thistle, symbolizes bravery, courage, loyalty, determination, and strength in the face of treachery or difficulty. These are qualities that stand a translator in good stead. The thistle has sharp prickles; translation is not for the thin-skinned or faint-hearted. Rubem Fonseca once joked in his off-color way that I was a "cu de ferro" (loosely translated as "lead butt," someone who can stick to a task for a long time—not to be confused with "hard-ass" or "badass"!). It's in character that I should be spending long hours working in the sunroom of Thistle Cottage, preparing classes and translating. Translation work requires considerable perseverance, patience, and consistency. The text before us is like a puzzle whose pieces must fit together seamlessly to create another whole with internal consistencies, even if they are incongruous. This takes time and care. The puzzle must be solved in a coherent way so that its meaning becomes clear to the beholder. Often, finding solutions to the puzzle requires a certain agility and the ability to work around a problem to come up with a viable solution. The quality of devotion is not slavish subservience but rather devotion to the art itself, which requires practice, like any art. We become skilled at it through repetition, false starts, and trial and error.

Reframing the Question: Loyalty and Betrayal

The old trope *tradutore/traitore* is a false binary that the contemporary translator roundly rejects. A fine work of literary translation is a feat of creative writing. In translating creatively, we betray expectations of the text and the language we are writing into. Writers bring all their working languages into their creative expression, creating unique word combinations, styles, and rhythms. People are obsessed with fidelity, and yet the passages where we are perhaps most "unfaithful" as translators are the most interesting, creative, and convincing. More important is the question of what we are to be faithful to. As translators, we search for meaning and the words to express it. We might find our own mode of expression through the language of the other. In any case, the very act of writing is one of exploring the potential of human languages. The "other voice" created by the translator can have a life outside the original. Most translators are bilingual or multilingual, and we bring a sort of creative contamination into our work. Gregory Rabassa said that it is not translators but words that are treacherous. Suzanne Jill Levine shows how words can manipulate and subvert, and the act of challenging words is what we do when we translate. Sub-version, she points out, is the "version underneath," and this is what the translation reveals. Sawako Nakayasu uses the moniker "errant translator" to describe those who resist pressure from the publishing world to produce something that will "sell" in exchange for taking risks of all kinds. We take different risks and convey a range of emotional registers when communicating in and from different languages. Recent science has proved that languages we learn create distinct neural pathways in the brain. Brain scans reveal that speakers of different languages have dense network connections within different hemispheres of the brain (Wei et al. 2023). Native speakers of German have strong white-matter networks in the left hemisphere, while native speakers of Arabic have denser networks bridging the two hemispheres. The roots of Arabic words, trios of consonants that connect to vowel patterns, require extra effort from parts of the brain that parse sounds and words. German has a complex and flexible word order that creates meaning by moving the place of words in a phrase. Learning a new language can stimulate interaction between brain hemispheres. It also changes other regions of the brain so that those with multiple language experiences may process nonlanguage information differently from those who speak only one language.

When we translate, we can feel the tone and register of the source language. When I am translating into English, I take risks with syntax, with diction, with word choice. From the Portuguese, I play with intimacy, humor, and vulgar language. Thinking in German, my first language, makes me feel like a young child, and I relive the emotions that it brings up of my relationships with the German-born side of my family. This complex language and its structure also influenced my own need for structure and nuance in my life. Portuguese is the language of my adolescence and early adulthood. Spanish is always linked to my experiences living in Colombia for five and a half years and honing my Spanish through teaching at the Universidad Javeriana in Bogotá, an institution known for its academic rigor. English is the language of my adulthood and professional life. People perceive us differently when we communicate in our different languages. We become another person in each language we speak; the language itself transforms us, shaping our inflections, cadence, and gestures. The contemporary Icelandic writer Hallgrímur Helgason ascribes vivid characteristics to different languages in his novel *Woman at 1,000 Degrees* (trans. Brian FitzGibbon, 2018) through the voice of his feisty narrator, a woman who lived in Iceland, the United States, and Europe in the pre- and post–World War II years and who had to survive by learning multiple languages:

> We Icelanders . . . walk around with gold in our mouths, a fact that has shaped us more than anything else. At least we don't squander words unnecessarily. . . . German strikes me as the least pretentious language, and its people use it the way a carpenter uses a hammer, to build a house for thought, although it can hardly be considered attractive. Apart from Russian, Italian is the most beautiful language in the world and turns every man into an emperor. French is a tasty sauce that the French want to savor in their mouths as long as possible, which is why they talk in circles and want to ruminate on their words, which often causes the sauce to dribble out of the corners of their mouths. Danish is a language the Danes are ashamed of. They want to be freed of it as soon as possible,

which is why they spit out their words. Dutch is a guttural language that gulped down two others. Swedish thinks it's the French of the north, and the Swedes do their utmost to relish it by smacking their lips. Norwegian is what you get when a whole nation does its best not to speak Danish. English is no longer a language but a universal phenomenon like oxygen and sunlight. Then Spanish is a peculiar perversion of Latin that came into being when a nation tried to adapt to a king's speech impediment, and yet it is the language I learned the best. (56)

The idea that language is a pristine sphere, or that it can be betrayed through translation, is not relevant to the multilingual world that we live in. Officially monolingual societies are for the most part socially engineered and reflect a national worldview and agenda (think of Nazi Germany, the United States, France). Most families in the world speak more than one language. English-speaking monolinguals are a tiny minority of those who speak English globally, including citizens and residents of the United States. It is humbling to learn and live in another language. When humility and respect for languages and cultures are not present, the world is impoverished, and peace is threatened. When we release expectations and accept living in a new language and culture as a beginner, the world awaits. The false argument (which has persisted for centuries) that translation is ultimately an act of betrayal distorts the fundamental question of what translation is and does. Translation is the ultimate alchemy of multiplying the communicative potential of language. It is resistance and errancy and subversion in the best, creative sense.

Piano Lessons

My parents were adamant that I learn a musical instrument and sought piano teachers for me everywhere we lived. My mother played the cello, and my parents were avid concertgoers. During our summers in Woodstock, New York, my parents signed me up for lessons with the late Hans Aldo Schimmerling (1900–1967), the Czech-born pianist, composer, and musicologist who lived in Woodstock. I found him to be an intimidating taskmaster, unforgiving and exhibiting old-school impatience (and arrogance) when my performance at the lesson did not meet his expectations. However, he was known for his contributions to music education in the schools until his retirement in 1960. I had many other piano teachers. My favorite was the lovely Dona Solange, who taught me in Rio and helped me feel comfortable with the instrument and performance. Listening to music was, I believe, my best teacher. My father had a shortwave radio that he would turn on every night, wherever we were, to listen to concerts broadcast from Europe and the United States. The sound was poor, often interrupted by static or long moments of silence, but it brought the world into our remote living rooms. I was not a gifted music student (I am thrilled that my granddaughters are proficient with the saxophone and the bass clarinet, respectively). What I took from those years of lessons was the importance of practice, perseverance, and the rich complexity of the language of music. My experience of learning to read music, and the habit of listening to a wide range of musical genres throughout my childhood and adolescence, prepared me well for working with the music of words on a page. While my piano lessons stopped after I graduated from high school—my last "act" was playing the piano solo for *Rhapsody in Blue* for a high school concert in Rio—what I carried forward was an appreciation of what it takes to excel in any art form. I still listen to words as I read them, and it is a practice that I hope I am teaching to my students.

Fahrvergnügen: The Joy of Travel and Traveling Through Translation

Travel is a privilege, and I have always felt most energized when contemplating or beginning a trip. My father felt the same way. His bright blue eyes would light up when he was planning the next adventure, and he would be ready and waiting, bags packed, impatient to get underway. Travel was something we did together throughout his life—sometimes just he and I. His excitement was contagious, and he taught me that a travel experience was a far greater gift than material possessions. Travel is a feeling of something experienced. It brings learning and connection. Travel generates story writing and storytelling. Travel is joy and catalyst. Travel is healing.

Translation is travel. The experience of travel can be given and received through the written word, which opens new geographies and horizons for writer and reader through the translator as medium. Susan Sontag says that translation is the circulatory system of the world. To me, travel quickens my blood and gives me energy, and the experience of travel feeds my translations. Fernando Pessoa reminds us that we can travel while in an armchair in our room. Elizabeth Bishop shows us that itineraries can be altered if we fall in love along the way. Clarice Lispector recalls that we can wander and not become lost. When we are back home, the emotions and experiences of the trip have become part of our DNA. We are forever altered and strengthened for the next adventure.

My Life Translated

One of my early childhood memories is waiting at a bus stop, holding my mother's hand, in bomb-ravaged Nuremberg, Germany, in 1951. I was four years old and about to start preschool at a German kindergarten. I remember the looming wreckage of ancient buildings all around me, their skeletons soaring skyward, and rubble in the streets. The reconstruction efforts had begun, but there was still haunting evidence of the destruction of war. I felt very small and vulnerable. Soon a van that served as a school bus came along, and my mother dried my tears and encouraged me to climb aboard. This was my first of many journeys into schools teaching in languages other than English. As a child being raised in German and English, it felt both familiar and formidable to me. My tears were not only of fright at being separated from my home but also of apprehension at what this unfamiliar world of a German classroom might hold. What were the rules? Even as a little girl, I knew there were codes and rules I had to learn to function in the new environment. From then on, I wanted to access those codes, to discover the patterns and rules that governed communication.

The rules of the world order were changing during the postwar years that I lived in Germany. The Allied powers were renegotiating the terms of peace for a postwar world. In his Four Freedoms speech of January 1941, President Franklin D. Roosevelt spoke of a new and more just world, a world with freedom of speech and expression, freedom of religion, freedom from want, and freedom from fear. In the Atlantic Charter later that year, he and Winston Churchill drafted a world order based on the principles of collective security, national self-determination, and free trade among nations. The United Nations was established, along with the World Bank, the International Monetary Fund, and the General Agreement on Tariffs and Trade. While much of what Roosevelt hoped for did not come about, it was surely a step forward for international relations that such institutions were created and largely accepted and, equally important, that they were underpinned by notions of a common humanity possessing the same universal rights. The idea that there were universal standards to be upheld was present, no matter how imperfectly, in the war crimes trials, and it was later reinforced by the establishment of the United Nations itself in 1945 and the International Court of Justice in 1946, as well as the Universal Declaration of Human Rights of 1948.

The Nuremberg trials were setting precedents for accountability for war crimes and establishing ground rules for the protection of human rights. The trials also inaugurated a new era for elevating the importance of translation and interpretation as fundamental to the communications required for world peace. The trials were personally significant to our family. My great-grandmother Helena Bromberg (b. 1862) and her son Robert were taken on September 15, 1942, by transport I/65, no. 6685, to Terezin and from there on September 29, 1942, by transport Bs, no. 264, to the east—to an "unknown destination," according to a June 6, 1949, letter from the Czech Ministry of the Interior to my great-aunt Elly Flynn, then residing in Beverly Hills, California. The letter stated, "Transport Bs is one of the death transports." Tom Stoppard's play *Leopoldstadt* is a family drama that echoes what happened to mine. Some family members saw the urgency to emigrate; others, like my grandmother and some of the family members in the play, refused to acknowledge what was coming. It is almost certain that Helene and Robert were killed at Auschwitz, one of the Nazi extermination camps in occupied Poland. I recently visited Dachau on a trip to Germany in September 2023. The background given by our knowledgeable Irish guide, who spoke with great tact and respect for the place we were visiting, taught me much that I didn't know about the camps and their functions. The horror of the genocide perpetrated by the Nazis struck me with full force, and I realized at that moment that the evil they perpetrated has not only affected the lives of multiple generations but will continue to do so as the world faces the threat of neo-Nazism. The great lesson of the camps, which are now open to visitors, is a warning: never forget. Protect and breathe life into our fragile democracies, and do not allow such crimes against humanity to occur ever again.

My grandparents had homes in Berlin and Munich and a modest summer chalet in the tiny town of Ohlstadt in Bavaria, near the Austrian border in the foothills of the Alps. These properties were confiscated by the Nazis, and my family never received restitution, despite efforts by my father and aunt. There was some loophole that prevented them from receiving compensation because of their immigration and naturalization status at the time they pursued the matter. Clarissa Daser, who was my nanny when we lived in Germany and who is now a vigorous ninety-eight-year-old, accompanied me to Ohlstadt on my many visits there throughout the years. My father had invited her to live with us in Nuremberg after the war, and he sponsored her US citizenship and her training as a US Army nurse. She recalled my grandparents and how my grandmother Alice—an elegant, charming woman, by Clarissa's description—would buy groceries at Clarissa's father's grocery store and take "loans" from Herr Daser to supplement her pocket money; he would add a few items to the "bill" to cover up the transaction. My grandfather, when he went to pay the bill, would marvel at the amount of the invoice but settled it with a gallant smile, probably knowing what was afoot. Clarissa described him as a tall, gregarious fellow who would treat everyone he met as an equal and who had a great sense of humor and a deep belly laugh. My great-grandmother Helena would spend summers at the villa in Ohlstadt, and my aunt Mady (a nickname for little girl in German, whose given name was Charlotte Elizabeth) would comb her hair in the garden. My father and aunt would spend the summers of their youth hiking and swimming in the nearby lakes with their Munich friends. We have a painting of my father at age fourteen, dressed in his lederhosen, and photographs of that golden time of innocence before their flight to freedom and a new, unknown future. On a recent visit to Ohlstadt, we were told in a matter-of-fact way by our German friends that the village was very homogeneous and that there were no Jews living there now. I was dismayed that there was so little trace or acknowledgment of the Jewish citizens who had lived there before 1933. This is not true in many other parts of Germany, where there are many memorials to the Jewish people as well as excellent museums (notably the Jewish Museum in Berlin) and reminders in public spaces of the history of their persecution.

My father, whose identity was transformed from a young university-educated art historian and designer to a Jewish Holocaust refugee to the United States, emigrated in 1934. After living in the United States for a few years, he was employed by the US government to serve as a researcher for the prosecution for the Nuremberg trials, although he did not start this job until 1947, when the trials were over. He must have been completing the research for the prosecution of the war crimes. He was subsequently assigned to the US adjutant general's office in Germany until 1952, most likely doing background checks on Germans as the civil government was reestablished. This was a result of his father's connections. My grandfather Alfred Schlomann, a renowned industrial engineer and technical writer who authored the well-known *Technical Dictionaries in Six Languages* (1910–40), emigrated to the United States in 1938 and was subsequently sent to advise the US strategic air command on the bombing of Germany during the war and its postwar reconstruction. My father was assigned to Nuremberg in 1947, the year my Brooklyn-born mother, Eleanor Allen, was pregnant with me, and he spent the nine months of my gestation in Nuremberg working and preparing for our arrival. (It is a vexing irony that my mother's parents were anti-Semitic and insisted that my father "convert" to the Episcopal Church.) They were married at the Columbia University Chapel in 1943. This never seemed to bother my father, however, who to his credit was always able to compartmentalize the painful experiences he had suffered and enjoy the good things in life with a sense of humor. In December 1947, my mother and I were flown on a DC-4 military transport plane to Germany, and we remained there until 1952. We were greeted by my father in the freezing cold the night before Christmas. He was allowed to ascend the staircase from the tarmac to the plane, where my mother appeared at the door, holding me in her arms. She handed me to my father with a sigh of relief after the twenty-two-hour trip via Gander (Newfoundland), Shannon (Ireland), and London to Frankfurt. The heating system on the plane had broken down and my mother covered me with her fur coat, which left her shivering. My parents collected our baggage and headed to the train station for the night train to Nuremberg. When we arrived at 2:00 am we were met by my father's friend Irwin Kent, a US Army captain, who stood on the platform in uniform to greet us. He drove us in his military jeep to the little house in Altenberg that had no central heating, just wood stoves in each room, outside the Nuremberg city limits. When we arrived at the door, Clarissa stood there in her German nurse's uniform and cap to receive us, and she took me in her arms. Standing next to her was our young German shepherd, Arras, who was professionally trained as a watchdog. He had gone through three stages of training as a protective dog. Each stage ended with a trial that included climbing over high barriers with wooden weights in his fangs, finding a hidden person in the woods and preventing him from escaping, learning how to fend off an attacker, and obeying complex commands. He earned the pedigree of *angekörte* (certified) guard dog and breeder. My parents would leave me in a baby carriage in front of stores with Arras on watch, feeling secure that nobody could approach us. Arras became my constant companion through our world travels until he died in my arms in Brazil at a ripe old age.

My dual Jewish-Anglican heritage was imprinted on me early. The displacement that my father, paternal aunt, and grandparents experienced became our continuing destiny. We would never know the stability of growing up in one place and belonging to a fixed community. I learned the importance of living multilingually. Family stories, traditions, and history from my Jewish grandparents, aunt, and father, along with my grandfather's work in multilingual terminology studies, sparked my interest in words and their contexts. My grandfather, whose life's work was codifying the terminology of emerging industries in six world languages and advocating for the standardization of terminology as a tool for global development, was also a wonderful raconteur who passed along tales of his life and adventures to his children—and to me. He wrote me sweet letters from New York when I was a toddler in Nuremberg. In one dated January 15, 1949, he wrote about dictionaries in response to a letter I had written (with my mother's help) with all the words I was learning in English and German.

Referring to my letter, my grandfather wrote:

> Your first dictionary edition does ease tremendously my conversations with you because now your answers and points of view are much clearer to me than before. Moreover, your very well picked out *termini technici* brought to my mind the merits of a thoroughly elaborated vocabulary. Before I became acquainted with your achievement, I did not consider such a compilation of great value; therefore, I thought a great deal of fuss was made about dictionaries. But now, I know I took a wrong view of this cause. There can be no doubt that everybody who feels inclined to express his flights of thought or wants to hide his lack of ideas should represent a special dictionary to reach understanding and agreement with a third party. Such procedure will and could avoid much trouble, e.g. between children and parents, or between oneself and members of his or her family, between girl- and boyfriends, or even between wife and husband. You know what I am aiming at. Moreover, I am certain if the ugly Nazis would have prepared a dictionary of their distorted Nazi-German language, everybody would have comprehended what they are talking about, they never would have gained their powerful position. Now, I must finish my letter, however, I have every wish to cultivate our correspondence which may prove mutually advantageous for our research as to philology. . . . To yourself, dear Elizabeth Anne, 99.9% of my love and countless kisses, Your Alfa-OPA.

My father carried forward his father's gift for storytelling, and in his later years he wrote about his life in pre- and postwar Europe. I helped him with this task and we self-published his book, titled *It's a Great Life*, in 1989. My grandfather, father, and aunt were proficient in English prior to emigrating to the United States; my grandmother, a professional singer, spoke German, English, French, and Italian, and she traveled throughout Europe giving performances. My father, as a prank with a friend, made up an invented language, and as a child I delighted in listening to them perform it for company. My mother learned to speak German fluently after marrying my father and knew Italian and French. An Equity actress, she spent many years working in children's theater and wrote stories, poems, and essays. Living overseas most of my life in the decades before the Internet, often in remote locations, led to a focus on reading. My parents transported a growing library to their various overseas homes, and my free time was spent with their books. Reading, writing, word games, puns, and language puzzles became my lifelong passions. In terms of my religious upbringing, my mother raised us in whatever version of the Episcopal church was available where we were, and if that was not available, we attended the interdenominational churches for the expatriate community. My aunt Mady married Marcel Loeb, a Belgian Jewish gentleman, after her emigration to New York. They kept a Jewish household and belonged to Congregation Habonim in New York, which was founded by Jewish émigrés, many of whom had experienced Nazi persecution. Through them and their vast network of friends and colleagues, I was schooled in Jewish customs, marked holidays, and made occasional visits to their synagogue on the Upper East Side, where my aunt's life was celebrated when she passed away at age ninety-five.

The Schlomann Dictionaries

My gregarious, fun-loving grandfather Alfred Schlomann (1878–1952) had an outsized influence on the development of my career. In addition to his work as a management consultant in Europe for emerging industries, he developed and pursued a massive project pioneering terminology management and documentation. The history of this work led to my developing graduate courses in the subject, and it shaped my approaches to both my translation practice and my teaching. He focused my attention on the critical importance of context in determining the correct equivalents of words, and he emphasized how words have resonances, registers, and multiple meanings, depending on how they are used. Wordsmithing is one of the most important tasks of the translator, and finding the right word is the product of deep familiarity with the working languages of the translator, finely honed research skills, and subject matter competence. The literary translator must be a linguist, etymologist, and poet to truly wield words effectively. My grandfather's work led to my connection with Sue Ellen Wright, who was a professor at Kent State University when I founded the translation program at the University of Florida in 2000. I had approached her for assistance with developing a course in terminology for my program, and when I told her that Alfred Schlomann was my grandfather, she hooted with delight. Her foundational work with Gerhard Budin in terminology management was indeed a continuation of the work started by Schlomann in the early twentieth century. I was gobsmacked when I connected the dots between my grandfather's work and the professional path I was already forging. We eventually presented together on Schlomann's project at a conference in Bergamo, Italy, in 2005 and coauthored a paper on his life and work.

As we reported in that paper, Schlomann received a degree and later an honorary doctorate at the Berlin Technische Hochschule in mechanical and industrial engineering. He studied banking and finance at the Universities of Berlin and Rostock. This prepared him to work with emergent industries, to analyze why they were failing, and to recommend measures to stimulate productivity. He was active for more than twenty-five years as a consulting engineer to more than one hundred companies, working in countries then known as Germany, France, Italy, Austria, Czechoslovakia, Poland, the Free State of Danzig, Romania, Hungary, Bulgaria, and Palestine. The sectors he addressed included machinery and machine tools, airplane manufacturing, steel, oil, plastics, the automotive industry, textiles, paper and wood, gas and gas engines, agricultural machinery, and glassworks, among others. His work embraced the financial and operations divisions in commercial and industrial enterprises, and he made important contributions to raising standards of efficiency through management techniques derived from scientific formulas and financial modeling. His activities included an examination of administrative and management operations, workforce organization, wage policies, procurement of raw materials, and workflow management. Schlomann's system of economic research and his setting of standards for industrial production have been widely recognized. His "break-even point" theory and its accompanying geometric formulas, which he elegantly termed the "geometry of returns" (Schlomann 1940, 50), is a benchmark in modern business economics. Because of this contribution and others, he has been credited with introducing a new science of industrial management. His economic theories can be linked to those of Frederick Taylor, who in 1911 published *The Principles of Scientific Management*, in which he described how the scientific management of workers could improve productivity. Both Taylor and Schlomann can be considered precursors to globalization, because they recognized that modern industry was leading the world to universal standards of production and borderless economies. Working in economics at the same time that Albert Einstein was revolutionizing human understandings of the universe and the relationship of parts to the whole, Schlomann and Taylor brought the scientific method to the industrial workplace. Schlomann took this a step further by linking standardization in the workplace to the standardization of terminology. His highly pragmatic implementation of terminology reflects a thoroughly grounded—and, for his time, highly innovative—theory of terminology management.

The genesis of Schlomann's twenty-one volumes of specialized terminology arose from his internship with the Verein Beratender Ingenieure (VBI) as a student in Berlin in 1905. VBI had started a dictionary project and invited Schlomann to work on it. As he labored on this project, he conceived of a radically different type of dictionary that could serve the needs of industry in an international context. The vision inspiring the dictionaries was that productivity was closely linked to accurate terminology management, particularly in new fields (such as aeronautics) that had not yet developed universal standards. The need for special subject dictionaries in multiple languages was a novel concept. The languages chosen for the project were German, English, Russian, French, Italian, and Spanish, reflecting the industrial economy of the interwar period. Schlomann organized the dictionaries systematically, with illustrations and alphabetical indexes in each language, so that translation was possible from each of the six languages into any of the others. The multilingual index contains an alphabetical key for each language, referring to the entry and page numbers. Eugen Wüster noted that when Schlomann published a dictionary of machine parts with a systematic structure in 1906, "this epoch-making achievement was first attacked and then celebrated" (2004, 298).

Schlomann's supporters in the financing and development of the massive dictionary project were convinced by his vision. Oldenbourg Publishers in Munich agreed to take on the project, and Schlomann was able to raise financing from heads of state, companies, and institutions. He organized the project as if it were an industrial enterprise. He created a company called Technische Worterbücher Verlag, GMbH. His headquarters was a large apartment in Munich that had been renovated out of two adjoining apartments. There he housed his typists and secretaries. He invented a typewriter with an oversized carriage to accommodate the layout of the terms and their definitions in table format in the six languages. His team grew to more than one thousand people in seven countries around Europe and South America, including linguists, translators, draftsmen, proofreaders, and subject matter specialists. Their work was done by correspondence over the thirty-four years that the project was underway (1906–40).

The rights to the dictionaries were taken away coercively from my grandfather by the Nazi regime and assigned by the Reichsschrifttumskammer to Dr. Walter Eppner by placing Eppner's name on the title pages of the printed and internationally distributed books between 1933 and 1945. After his emigration to the United States in 1938, Schlomann worked tirelessly to recover his copyright and royalties. The dictionaries had been "vested" by the US government in 1943 and "held in the interest and for the benefit of the United States." A total compensation of $250 was paid to the Schlomann family for royalties upon the restitution of copyright and the release of the books after the war. Meanwhile, Schlomann served the US government in the strategic reconstruction of Germany, leveraging his in-depth knowledge of European industry for the purposes of building peace and a new Europe. Contemporary world events confirm his early vision of globalization, with the rise of the European Union and regional trading blocs spanning hemispheres, and the need for industry- and discipline-specific terminology continues to grow.

Schlomann's fundamental contribution to modern terminology management is his realization that the documentation of product- and process-related terminology is relevant to the success of core business activity. Although this principle underlies broad areas of internationalization and localization today, it is still not universally recognized throughout industry. His work as an industrialist, engineer, and terminologist also prefigures the careers of Eugen Wüster and, later, of the special language lexicographer Richard Ernst. In comparison to Ernst, who took a more traditional lexicographical approach to German-English technical vocabulary, Schlomann made a significant step into the semantic representation of linguistic information by presenting a kind of concept orientation that has become the hallmark of terminology management in multilingual environments.

The logistical scope of Schlomann's undertaking, which predates the advent of computerization and electronic communications, is amazing, considering that he created a pre-computer age infrastructure to undertake his ambitious project. Today's localization environments work with up to forty languages and utilize a wide variety of computational tools. Schlomann's efforts to create his own typewriters prefigure the development of software solutions, multilingual typefaces and fonts, and Unicode script representation in today's computing spaces. It is difficult to compare Schlomann's organizational enterprise to current terminology management undertakings within the framework of major governmental initiatives (e.g., Canada's Termium or the European Union's Eurodicautom resources) or ongoing in-house efforts such as Microsoft's localization-oriented, contextually linked terminology files or IBM's hybrid lexicography/terminology resources. These efforts have been implemented through the investment and commitment of nations and of the world's largest companies, whereas Schlomann's accomplishments reflect the entrepreneurial zeal of a single individual and his ability to inspire powerful supporters to underwrite his venture. His approach to linguistic knowledge organization not only remains viable but promises to provide future researchers with the tools to create more advanced knowledge management resources.

Port-au-Prince, Haiti

Auditory and olfactory memories abound of our years in Haiti, where we lived after three years in Washington, DC, following the Nuremberg assignment. In our lovely sprawling house in Pétion-Ville, with its wrought-iron window bars and what seemed to my child's eyes miles of tile floors, I would hear the call and response of Vodou drums every night from the mountains surrounding our home, to the accompaniment of the frogs and the insects humming deep-throated chants. I smelled the acrid smoke of charcoal fires in the servants' quarters outside the house and the dense fragrance of tropical foliage in the hot, humid night air. My favorite pastime was climbing the tree in our yard and watching the exotic lizards inflate their brilliantly colored air sacs. I had a view of the grounds, the outside gate, and the surrounding hills. I could watch the foot traffic on the dirt road outside our gate; women carrying bundles and jugs on their heads, their babies strapped to their backs; and the riotously colorful minibuses (tap-taps) bursting to capacity with people and livestock. On Saturdays I would accompany my mother to the open-air market in the center of Pétion-Ville, a ten-minute walk from our house. Intense smells emanated from the produce, livestock, and crowds of people. The melodic sounds of spoken, shouted, and sung Haitian Creole filled the air. We filled our baskets with bananas, avocadoes, mangoes, lemons, papayas, passion fruit, yams, tomatoes, onions, carrots, spinach, fresh bread and rolls, and paper packets of rice and beans. I learned to bargain with the vendors and pay them in Haitian gourdes, handing the change to my mother. Donkeys laden with firewood plodded along the sides of the street. At home, we unloaded the baskets in the large airy kitchen presided over by Flavitte, the cook. She would keep us children in line when my parents were away by demonstrating her "special" powers (she would make objects disappear and then reappear in unlikely places) and ventriloquism, projecting her voice into cupboards and under beds. These skills kept us enthralled and on our best behavior. I liked nothing more than to be invited to the servants' quarters and listen to them tell stories and sing over the cooking fire, from which delicious smells of goat stew, rice, and beans wafted, and to watch the "laundry lady" iron clothes with the heavy, coal-heated iron. Having domestic servants was a reality of expatriate living and common to wealthier families in those days, and it still is in many countries. As a child I spent hours conversing with them wherever we lived, and they were the source of much of my local knowledge and language learning. I grew to love and respect them, and their stories have remained with me to this day.

I attended the Union School in downtown Port-au-Prince, which was located a few blocks away from the National Palace on the Avenue de la République, then the residence of the president of Haiti. The students gathered every morning on the patio in front of the school to sing the Haitian national anthem in French and the US national anthem in English. Our instruction was in English and French. My mother taught at the school. After school she would drive me to ballet and piano lessons in downtown Port-au-Prince or to play dates with my best friend, Carol St. John, whose father also worked there for the US State Department. Our life was, on the surface, peaceful. My parents became active in the community and befriended local artists and musicians, often entertaining them in our home. Among them was Félix Morisseau-Leroy (1912–1998), the Haitian writer and playwright who wrote in Creole and was responsible for having Creole recognized as an official language of Haiti. He expanded the teaching of the language in schools and its use in creative writing. He was later exiled from Haiti and moved to Africa. Wilson Bigaud (1931–2010) was another occasional guest, and my parents acquired several of his paintings. Born into poverty, he studied at Port-au-Prince's Centre d'Art, established by the American artist DeWitt Peters. Bigaud soon earned a reputation as one of Haiti's major painters; his subjects were the common people, depicted in vivid color and movement. My mother joined the Holy Trinity Episcopal Cathedral in downtown Port-au-Prince, which was known for its beautiful murals by Haitian artists depicting biblical scenes with Haitian subjects, affirming an alternative view of the dominant Caucasian depiction of Jesus and other biblical figures. (The cathedral was destroyed in the 2010 earthquake, and under the auspices of the Smithsonian Haiti Cultural Recovery Project, efforts began to recover and restore the murals for later placement in a reconstructed cathedral.) My memory of the place is from my role as an angel in Christmas pageants that were organized and staged by my mother in collaboration with the American nuns who worked there. I have photographs of myself standing in full angel regalia, with spread wings, in front of the mural that then stood behind the altar.

Occasionally we would spend weekends at the beach or, to escape the heat of the capital, take excursions to the Forêt des Pins, a forest in southeastern Haiti. It was an expanse of coniferous and subtropical plants, but it has been severely deforested. In the first years of the twentieth century, it consisted of thirty-two thousand hectares; today, only six thousand hectares remain. On one such visit, my little brother Rick was chasing his twin sister, Peggy, around the dining room table of our rented cabin and hit his head, cutting it badly. The only medical help available was a local veterinarian, who arrived smelling foully of Haitian rum. Terrified, I ran out into the forest while he sewed my brother's head up, hiding until he left and my brother's cries had subsided. Another traumatic event occurred the night before I was going to leave Haiti for my annual summer visit to my aunt Mady in New York. I was nine years old. My mother had packed my bag, and I was ready for my departure the next day. The morning I was to travel, I woke up, my head swimming and my vision blurred. I was vaguely aware of my parents' voices in the room, my mother's trained soprano voice rising over the others in a state of alarm. A doctor was checking my vital signs. When I regained consciousness, I was told that I had been robbed and drugged in the night by a thief who had slipped in through the burglar bars, leaving tracks of grease along the wall where he had dropped down into the room. This was apparently common practice; thieves were known to invade homes by covering their naked bodies in grease and squeezing through burglar bars. He had placed a rag doused in chloroform over my mouth, rendering me fully unconscious, and had also managed to drug Arras, the German Shepherd dog that slept on the floor in front of my room at night. The thief had taken everything in the room, including my packed suitcase. He had not ventured into the rest of the house, perhaps scared off by the dog's becoming restless or some other noise. After my parents were reassured that I was going to be fine and that my twin siblings in the next room were also unharmed, my mother sprang into action. She arranged for me to borrow clothing from my best friend, Carol, and I made it to the plane on time. My dear aunt was happy to rebuild my wardrobe on a few shopping trips to her favorite New York City stores, B. Altman and Bloomingdale's. When I returned to Haiti after a carefree summer spent in the Catskills with my aunt and uncle at their home in Woodstock, New York, I went with my mother back to the open-air market. I caught a glimpse of a little girl in a bright pink shorts-and-top outfit. She was wearing my stolen clothes! I cried out in indignation to my mother, who clamped my mouth shut with her hand, warning me not to say or do anything. She insisted that the little girl needed those clothes more than I did, and that was the end of the discussion.

Our time in Haiti came to a violent end. After a coup attempt against his regime in July 1958, François Duvalier disbanded the independent military and formed a rural militia called the Volunteers for National Security (Volontaires de la Sécurité Nationale, or VSN—more commonly known as the Tonton Macoutes, a name derived from the Creole term for a mythological bogeyman). Duvalier proceeded to expel Americans from Haiti, considering them a threat to his ambitions to flaunt democratic institutions and become president for life. One day in late 1958 the armed Tonton Macoutes surrounded the Union School, and we fled under gunfire. Parents rushed to the school to pick up their children. Carol's mother took me in her car, and we rode on the car floor to their house, where I stayed for a few days until it was safe to return to my own. By this time, my parents were packing up the house and making arrangements to evacuate on orders from the US State Department. In the wake of our departure, Duvalier's rule became entrenched. Known as Papa Doc because he had been a rural doctor in the provinces, Duvalier had studied Vodou practices and beliefs and was rumored to be a *houngan*. He related effectively to *houngan* and *bokò* (sorcerers) throughout the country and incorporated many of them into his intelligence network and the ranks of the Tonton Macoutes. His public recognition of the religion, which had originated in Dahomey and was then transformed by slaves on the island as a way of restoring a sense of identity and a force of liberation, enhanced his popular persona among the common people. (They also hesitated to trifle with a leader who allegedly had dark forces at his command.) It served as a peculiar form of legitimization for his rapacious rule. I have never returned to Haiti and have followed the country's misfortunes from afar with dismay as it has suffered through corrupt governments, natural disasters, and now the impunity of vicious gangs and drug trafficking. The languages, generosity, beauty, and creativity of the Haitian people have remained with me from childhood. Wilson Bigaud's evocative painting of a Vodou dance hangs in our living room.

The Brazil Years: Living in Portuguese

After leaving Haiti, where he had been with the Point Four Program, my father was assigned by the State Department to work in Brazil. He was now officially with the Agency for International Development (AID). It is public knowledge that USAID and the Central Intelligence Agency (CIA) had overlapping missions in South America during the Cold War, which were to further democracy and to support US businesses, especially large multinationals, regarding market access and the protection and furthering of their investments. These companies had strong influence over the CIA. Philip Agee's book *Inside the Company: CIA Diary* (1975), sheds light on the CIA mission in Brazil:

> It's all over for Goulart in Brazil much faster and easier than most expected. . . . U.S. recognition of the new military government is practically immediate, not very discreet but indicative, I suppose, of the euphoria in Washington now that two and a half years of operations to prevent Brazil's slide to the left under Goulart have suddenly bloomed.
>
> Our campaign against him took much the same line as the ones against communist infiltration in the Velasco and Arosemena governments two and three years ago in Ecuador. According to Holman [Ned Holman, CIA Chief of Station in Montevideo], the Rio station and its larger bases were financing the mass urban demonstrations against the Goulart government, proving the old themes of God, country, family, and liberty to be effective as ever. Goulart's fall is without doubt largely due to the careful planning and consistent propaganda campaigns dating at least back to the 1962 election operation. (361–62)

My father's work was in communications (Haiti and Brazil) and capital development (Brazil), functions that supported US government messaging and funneling of resources to organizations and individuals. His job was to support technicians who were delivering aid. In his communications role he set up displays and booths, supported conferences and road trips, arranged audiovisual equipment and recordings, rented space for the same, and perhaps even established liaisons with local media. My mother did a lot to serve as an unpaid cultural ambassador. She did this because she was a skilled cellist and actress and enjoyed participating as a contributing member of art communities, particularly music and theater. It is hard to judge whether the CIA ever used AID for its direct purposes, and it would not appear that my father was ever able to facilitate access to any contacts in whom the CIA would be interested. My parents were devoted to supporting the arts. They were highly educated and humanistic in their thinking, and I think they were really interested in assisting with development and not acting as Cold Warriors.

We traveled to Brazil on the Moore-McCormack ships that sailed between New York and South America starting in the 1920s. The "Good Neighbor Fleet"—a trio of ships named *Argentina*, *Brazil*, and *Uruguay*—was replaced in 1958 by newer, faster ships christened SS *Argentina* and SS *Brazil*. We were on the *Brazil* on our first voyage to Rio de Janeiro in 1959. The trip took almost two weeks, with a stop in St. Thomas. We landed in Rio de Janeiro on a hot, sultry January day and were housed in the then Miramar Hotel on Copacabana Beach. We were spending the month in Rio, during the Brazilian summer school break, before moving on to my father's first post in Curitiba, Paraná. We went to the beach every day and then escaped for a few weeks to a small resort hotel in Petrópolis for relief from the heat. There I had my first "urgent care" experience in Brazil: a large insect crawled into my ear in the middle of the night, causing excruciating pain that a local doctor relieved by flushing it out. My olfactory memory brings back the smells of the moist mountain air, the exotic tropical foliage, and the reddish earth. Elizabeth Bishop's poetry also conjures up that Petrópolis experience. She lived in Petrópolis at the Fazenda Samambaia with her Brazilian lover, Lota de Macedo Soares, the upper-class architect and socialite who designed and built Rio de Janeiro's Parque de Flamengo with the support of those in power in the military dictatorship. In her 1965 collection, *Questions of Travel*, which is dedicated to Lota, Bishop describes the house in "Song for the Rainy Season":

> Hidden, oh hidden
> in the high fog
> the house we live in,

beneath the magnetic rock,
rain-, rainbow-ridden,
where blood-black
bromelias, lichens,
owls, and the lint
of the waterfalls cling,
familiar, unbidden. (101–2)

Bishop and Macedo Soares's tumultuous love story, which unfolded in Petrópolis and Rio de Janeiro in the 1950s and '60s, ended badly, triggered in part by Macedo Soares's close ties with the conservative politician Carlos Lacerda, who was elected governor of Guanabara state in 1960 and offered her a position in his administration. Later, Macedo Soares socialized with members of the military regime, whom Bishop railed against at US embassy parties. Bishop left Brazil during the dictatorship, unable to reconcile herself to living in the country under the regime. In 1965, she accepted a position at the University of Washington. She returned to Brazil, to Ouro Preto, after Macedo Soares's suicide in New York in 1967, traveling back and forth between the United States and Brazil through 1974. Bishop published many poems set in Brazil and translated Brazilian poets Carlos Drummond de Andrade, João Cabral de Melo Neto, Joaquim Cardozo, and Manuel Bandeira. She was Clarice Lispector's neighbor at her apartment in Rio de Janeiro, and she translated three of Lispector's stories for the *Kenyon Review* in 1964. It was only later, of course, that I discovered how geographically close I had been to Bishop at the time, and she and her relationship with Brazil have been an inspiration to my development as a translator, reader, and writer. Brazil, for Bishop and for me, could possibly have been the closest thing to a real home. She met and socialized with the elite of Brazilian literary, artistic, and political circles. She also counted Americans living in Brazil as her friends. She traveled throughout the country and was fascinated by the sexual energy of the country, which freed her to live her life as an openly lesbian woman. In his wonderful 1991 article titled "Elizabeth Bishop and Brazil" in the *New Yorker*, Lloyd Schwartz comments that her poem "Pink Dog" offers the deepest insight into her complex relationship with Brazil, in which she reveals a "laughter of despair" about the country: "Having given up Brazil, she could finally become a Brazilian" (96).

> They say that Carnival's degenerating
> —radios, Americans, or something,
> have ruined it completely. They're just talking.
>
> Carnival is always wonderful!
> A depilated dog would not look well.
> Dress up! Dress up and dance at Carnival!

My mother cried in despair when we arrived in Curitiba, where we would live for the next two years. As we drove down the main street in a US government van, large enough to hold our family of seven and our luggage, she burst into tears. What we saw were small houses and buildings, some with colonial facades, few paved streets, and the ubiquitous Paraná pines dotting the landscape. We stopped in front of a modest building, the Hotel Johnscher, which would be our home until we found housing. The establishment was owned by a family of German descent, who installed us in a wooden three-bedroom house with a porch in the back of the hotel. The roof leaked, and when it rained, water would drip onto our beds. With twin infants (my brothers Rob and Fred), another set of five-year-old twins (Peggy and Rick), and me, age eleven, at what seemed like the back end of beyond, my mother felt unmoored. It was a while before she would sing and dance again.

The capital of the southern state of Paraná, Curitiba lies at about 3,050 feet near the Atlantic margin of the Brazilian Highlands and the headwaters of the Iguaçú River. It was founded in 1654 as a gold-mining camp, but the processing of mate and wood products brought long-term growth. In 1854 Curitiba became the state capital. For centuries, the city was little more than an outpost for travelers moving between São Paulo and the surrounding agricultural regions. Curitiba was the "sleeping city," a place where cattle drivers would shelter in the winter en route to their next destination. When a wave of European immigration hit southern Brazil, Curitiba's farmland was an obvious attraction. Germans arrived in the 1830s; Polish and Italians arrived in the 1870s; and Ukrainians came two decades later. Each group occupied a section of the city, developing its own local industries and beginning to populate the downtown area with churches, shops, and restaurants. The mechanization of soybean production pushed Paraná's agricultural workers off their land and into the city. Between 1940 and 1960, the city's population more than doubled—from 140,000 to 360,000 residents. Curitiba was quickly becoming the archetypal Brazilian midsize city. Favelas grew around its periphery; car traffic increased. In the 1960s, following the military coup in 1964, mayor Ivo Arzua put out a call for a master urban plan to manage Curitiba's growth. When Jaime Lerner (1937–2021), an architect, took over as mayor of the city for the first of three times in 1971, he began to implement a long-debated plan that radically transformed Curitiba into a world model for a green city, with an innovative low-fuel-emission transportation system, pedestrian walkways, expanded green spaces, and other improvements. The model has been celebrated and studied around the world. Despite continued growth and setbacks due to successive changes of administration, Curitiba is still the subject of urban planning research.

Curitiba was, at the time we moved there, still a provincial capital, with a small landowning and industrial upper class. It boasted a national library, a municipal theater, and the Universidade Federal de Paraná, which would later become central to my work in international education at the University of Florida. It was also the home of the then unknown Dalton Trevisan, whom I would later meet, befriend, and translate during my dissertation research on an Organization of American States (OAS) grant in 1976. Trevisan wrote of the Curitiba suburbs, and his signature book, *O vampiro de Curitiba* (1965; *The Vampire of Curitiba and Other Stories*, trans. Gregory Rabassa, 1972), spins lurid tales of sex and violence in the lower middle class.

My parents were insistent, as they had been in Haiti, that I learn the local language as quickly as possible. I was enrolled in the Colégio Martinus. Founded in 1948 as a *Gemeindeschule* by German immigrants, instruction was in German and Portuguese. We wore uniforms (brown skirts or trousers and a white shirt) and were seated in class from front to back according to our grades, with the worst students in the back. Paddling was accepted and used. Of course, I was relegated to the back of the room as a result of my linguistic confusion. I gradually learned Portuguese through German and succeeded in earning a seat in the front row. Instruction involved memorization and rote repetition of facts related to Brazilian history, geography, and literature, among other subjects. I rode on the public bus to the school in the mornings, and in the afternoons I worked on lessons in English for the Calvert correspondence course my mother enrolled us in (then a mail-in service) to keep us abreast of the US education system. Extracurriculars involved a home economics class at a community center and youth activities in the local expatriate interdenominational church that my mother had joined. I was also enrolled in the Bandeirantes, the national guiding organization of Brazil—a Brazilian version of the Girl Scouts. Founded in 1919, the coeducational organization became a full member of the World Association of Girl Guides and Girl Scouts in 1930. The name comes from the group of explorers who pushed into Brazil's interior from the coast to avoid pirates as well as the imperial bureaucracy. They have a mixed reputation in Brazil but are generally part of the mythology of Brazil's growth as a nation. My contribution to the Bandeirantes was to demonstrate the baking of an American apple pie.

My mother, always resilient and determined, regrouped and became involved in the community. She played cello in the symphony orchestra of the Universidade Federal and volunteered for women's groups. She found and befriended the doctor who would become our family physician and later gain fame as a proponent of incorporating Indigenous Brazilian health practices into Western medicine. Dr. Moysés Goldstein Paciornik (1914–2008) had founded the Paranaense Center for Medical Research in 1959 for cancer prevention and treatment and gynecological services that he offered to Indigenous people on reservations in southern Brazil, who were also the subjects of his research. He became a supporter of squatting birth, noting that the Kaingang Indian women had stronger vaginal muscles than Westerners owing to their squatting practices. When my husband, Terry, and I visited him on a trip to Brazil in the late 1990s, we visited the clinic, which had a sign at the elevator that read: "You wouldn't be here if you took the stairs." In his office, he regaled us with stories of his medical career while inviting us to squat as we talked. My memory of his treating me as a child was the time when I developed a boil on my hand. When he lanced it, I fainted dead away on the floor of his office. He laughed, as he remembered the incident as well, and spoke of fond memories of my mother. My parents also befriended the Chinese Brazilian painter Helena Wong (1938–1990), who lived in a cottage close to our house. She was a diminutive woman who suffered from a rheumatic disease that deformed her hands. We acquired several of her paintings and engravings. Later she went on to earn many prizes, and she participated in national and international exhibits in Brazil and abroad, including at the Museum of Modern Art in New York.

In 1961, my father was transferred to work in the US embassy in Rio de Janeiro. The move was timely, since I was about to start high school, and I was able to enroll in the Escola Americana (EA), an international school then located in Leblon. We moved into a spacious apartment on the Avenida Bartolomeu Mitre in a low-rise apartment building within walking distance of the school and the beach. This was the year that *Life* magazine sent American photographer Gordon Parks to report on poverty in Rio de Janeiro. The resulting piece, titled "Freedom's Fearful Foe: Poverty," was groundbreaking for its focus on the grinding poverty of the *favela*. The *favelas* were in sight of the picture windows of our apartment's living room. Our lives, by contrast, were privileged. Centered around school, my parents' work and activities, and weekend excursions to the beach or the surrounding rainforest and the higher elevations of Petrópolis, we immersed ourselves in all that *carioca* culture had to offer. By this time my Portuguese was native-speaker proficient, and I enjoyed the bilingual curriculum at EA. I took piano and dance lessons, navigated the city on my own by public bus, on foot, or by bike, and felt comfortable and at home. I was of course unaware that the writer who was to influence me deeply and become my compass in my work in translation and translation scholarship, Rubem Fonseca, lived a few short blocks away on Rua General Urquiza. Nélida Piñon also lived in Leblon at the time, and Clarice Lispector was at her apartment in Copacabana. I would later meet them all in person and develop close ties to them as a translator, scholar, and friend. My favorite classes were in language and literature. Mrs. Yindrisky Stekly, educated at the University of Prague, was a memorable, strict Latin teacher with hilarious mannerisms that provoked fits of laughter among her students; she had us act out the death of Julius Caesar in Latin every year, complete with fake blood. Madame Raymonde de Vasconcellos (University of Grenoble), the lovely French teacher, drilled us in pronunciation and French etiquette while instilling in us a love of the classics of French literature. Dona Nadyr (Naná) Collares (University of Brazil) taught us advanced Portuguese and wielded her irrepressible sense of humor—and drill-sergeant discipline—to insist on proper grammar and command of vocabulary. My downfall was mathematics. It was thanks to the tutelage of kind Dr. Rupert Fox (Pontificia Universidade Catolica) that I made it through four years of math. With my sidekick Carol (C.J.) Gerbracht, I was delegated to collect some of the pithy class remarks by the trigonometry teacher, Peter Gurau (Harvard), for our yearbook, including "I get the feeling I've lost you," "All mathematics is redundant," "Please remember it's quite obvious," and "Let's postulate the impossible on the ridiculous."

In 1963, my father was again transferred, this time to the USAID mission in Recife. The 1961 Foreign Assistance Act under the new Kennedy administration focused on addressing organizational problems perceived in previous foreign-assistance programs and led to long-term development planning on a country-by-country basis. One of the first programs under USAID was the Alliance for Progress, which became the basis for USAID programs in the 1960s. My father worked in this organization, which also operated as an umbrella for CIA activities focused on funding and promoting anti-Communist activities. My mother had arranged for me to live with her close friend and neighbor, Dona Olympia, who became my Brazilian surrogate mother and a major role model in my life. At that time, Recife had no organized international school, and my parents wanted me to finish high school in Rio. Dona Olympia, a sociologist, was one of the first women to become a full professor at the Federal University of Rio de Janeiro. Cultivated, beautiful, and fluent in Portuguese, Italian, and English, she maintained a gracious home in the apartment next to ours with her two daughters (one adopted) and her Portuguese maid. She was also the mistress and common-law wife of a wealthy Brazilian industrialist whom I knew as Dom Carvalho. Dom Carvalho would come for dinner twice or three times a week, a formal affair served by the Portuguese maid in full uniform. Dona Olympia, a well-informed conversationalist, insisted on discussing topics of national and international interest and matters of culture and the arts. After dinner, she would ask me to play the piano. She and Dom Carvalho treated me like a daughter and would regularly take me out to the theater, to concerts, and to dinner. When I was getting ready for my senior prom, Dona Olympia hired her seamstress to make me a beautiful gown made of white raw silk, which she supervised with care and an eye for Parisian fashion. It was she who introduced me to Jorge Amado. She presented me with the first edition of *Dona Flor e seus dois maridos* (1966) when I returned to Brazil from college on a visit to my parents, who had been reassigned to Rio. I came to realize how much Olympia and Carvalho's story had impacted my understanding and appreciation of the fluidity and resilience of Brazilian culture and society, its tolerance for ambiguity, and its embrace of the joys of love in all its forms without judgment. Olympia died of breast cancer in the late 1970s, and I received a touching note from Dom Carvalho with the news.

During the time I lived with Dona Olympia, the military coup occurred on March 31, 1964, at the end of my junior year. I was on a local bus at the time. I remember traffic coming to a full stop and tanks rolling out into the streets. We were held on the bus for hours. At that time, before cell phones, there was no way to contact either Dona Olympia or my family, far away in Brazil's northeast. When we were finally released from the bus, I remember walking all the way back to Leblon from Copacabana, since buses and taxis were prohibited from picking up passengers. In hindsight, I realize how fortunate I was to have made it back to the apartment without having been detained. The dictatorship began a dark period in Brazil that lasted for over twenty years. Books were banned; people were disappeared, incarcerated, and tortured; and cultural life ground to a painful halt. The military regime installed a tutelary authoritarian regime to control civil society and the political system, which became a model for similar regimes in Latin America during the Cold War—notoriously, Argentina and Chile. They created a military-industrial complex designed to accelerate capitalist development and the "integration" of Brazil's huge landmass. There was strong opposition from civil society, which reflected diverse ideological and social backgrounds: Marxists, liberals, socialists, progressive Catholics, artists, and intellectuals. They refused to negotiate with the military and their policies.

My time in Rio was spent in school and extracurricular music and dance classes during the week, and on weekends, at the beach or in Petrópolis with friends. My schoolmates and I were free to roam the city once "order and progress" had been established by the military regime, and favorite outings included Bob's (the franchise that sold US-style hamburgers and milkshakes) and the local movie theaters. Our rival in sports and debate was the Graded School in São Paulo, and we would go to São Paulo by bus for events. I was not athletic but did participate in the debate club and in chorus and theater. One of my favorite Rio haunts was the Jardim Botânico, where I collected insects for biology class and enjoyed walking through the park. Our high school graduation (class of 1965) was held at the American ambassador's residence in Rio, not far from the Jardim, and was an elegant affair attended by families and representatives of the diplomatic corps. There were only about sixty of us in the class, students of many different nationalities who scattered around the world after we parted. Many have stayed in touch to this day, thanks to email and social media. Our feelings for Rio and our life there as expatriate kids are summed up in these (anonymous) excerpts from our 1965 yearbook: "Beneath that sun-tanned surface, the pressure is on. Because EA is a college prep school, anxiety is a normal part of life. Work piles up. We admire the coolheaded kids who can take it without a panic. And it makes us appreciate much more those rare times when we can relax."

My high school classmate, Elisabeth Hallett (née Brutto), now a published poet, wrote:

Rio turns in her sleep and pours our footprints into the tide
and our sandcastles
and cigarette butts
and the beach is empty at sunrise
until we come back to taste summer again
or catch drops of it on our eyelashes
and all over our skin
burning, brown, and golden . . .

the way your sandals look
striding over the sidewalk
and how they sting a bit hot noonday silence
que bom
to feel like a young animal
with the sun glowing in your bones
even as you sit cool under the awning of a small
tin-tabled and fly-blown bar (Hallett 2003, 6)

I visited my family in Recife regularly during the two years I lived in Rio with Dona Olympia. The reason for the US government presence in the northeast had to do with perceived leftist influence in the region. Tad Szulc published an article in the *New York Times* on October 31, 1960, titled "Northeast Brazil Poverty Breeds a Threat of Revolt." He states, "The makings of a revolutionary situation are increasingly apparent across the vastness of the poverty-stricken and drought-plagued Brazilian Northeast. In the area 20,000,000 people live on average annual incomes of less than $100. Racked by chronic malnutrition and rampaging disease, they seldom live much beyond the age of thirty. The misery is exploited by the rising Leftist influences in the overcrowded cities. The Communist-infiltrated Peasant Leagues . . . have become an important political factor in this area" (Szulc 1960, 1). On one of my visits, a bomb was thrown into the offices where my father and colleagues worked in downtown Recife. I was there at the time, and I recall taking shelter under a government-issued metal desk.

Despite the undercurrent of political tensions and the obvious contradictions of our place as an American family in Recife, I grew to love the atmosphere and flavors of northeast Brazil, which would guide my translations of northeastern writers later. My parents first lived in Casa Amarela, near the Gilberto Freyre home, which is now the site of the Gilberto Freyre Foundation. The great sociologist was still living when I was spending time in Recife. Although I did not meet him in person, I visited the big house, which became the seat of his foundation, and I became well acquainted with his seminal works as an undergraduate at Barnard College in New York City and later in my academic career. In 1926, Freyre organized the first northeast congress in Recife and published the "Regionalist Manifesto" with other key figures at the time, the writers Jorge de Lima, José Américo de Almeida, José Lins do Rego, and others. His work is about the socioeconomic development of northeastern Brazil and the important role of Afro-Brazilians in the construction of a national identity. He strongly believed that Brazil's multicultural, multiracial society could serve as a model for the rest of the world. His analyses of the patriarchal landowning society, the relationship of Brazil's Portuguese colonizers and their African slaves, and the process of urbanization and the decline of the rural patriarchy are iconic contributions to our understanding of the complexity of race relations in Brazil. Knowledge of his writings has been key to my translations of three generations of Brazilian writers whose work focuses on the northeast.

Recife, capital of the state of Pernambuco, has been called the Venice of Brazil because the city is crossed by waterways and its various neighborhoods are linked by bridges. It was an epicenter of the sugar trade in the sixteenth century and raided by French and English pirates in the late 1500s. The Dutch captured the city in 1630 and ruled it for twenty-four years. The city became the capital of the province of Pernambuco in 1827. In the 1960s the region developed further, with the federal organization called Sudene (Superintendência para o Desenvolvimento do Nordeste) in collaboration with US government agencies. The city became a hub for northeastern popular and high culture, with its universities, research institutes, museums, and theaters. The Boa Viagem beach became a big tourist attraction; it is also a center of the sailing community. My husband, Terry, and I participated as crew on a friend's forty-seven-foot Swan in a sailing regatta from Recife to the island of Fernando de Noronha in 2007, and I hardly recognized the city when I returned more than forty years after my time there with my family. The Fernando de Noronha race was probably our greatest sailing adventure. Our carefully compiled list of sailing terminology deserted us completely during a storm in the middle of the night when Terry was at the helm. Our crewmates were screaming at him in Portuguese to turn into the wind, but in all the confusion he forgot the meaning of the words and had to be replaced at the helm. We wrote about the experience in an article we titled "Sailing as a Second Language" that was published in *Cruising World* magazine. Sailing indeed has its own language, one that I relished learning. I took a course titled Save the Captain to learn principles of navigation, boat safety and maintenance, and electronic communications. Filled with specialized terminology, sailing language is a fascinating mix of terms that originate from ancient mariner traditions along with the high-tech jargon of modern navigation using GPS with apps on a laptop or cell phone. Of all the languages I speak, sailing language is perhaps the one that gives me the most pride of accomplishment.

On one return to Recife in June 1966, at the end of my freshman year at Barnard College, a great flood inundated the city after torrential rains made the Capiberibe and Beberibe rivers overflow, displacing more than five hundred thousand people. The home we rented was close to the Capiberibe. We had to be evacuated by boat to higher ground. I accompanied my siblings Peggy and Rick, then age twelve, to the residence of a State Department family away on home leave. My parents went to another house with the younger twins, age eight. We managed for about three days with no water, phone, or electricity, foraging for food in the well-stocked pantry of the host family. After the waters subsided, our family had to move to another house in Boa Viagem, a neighborhood close to the ocean, since the flooded home could not be repaired in a reasonable time. When we went back into the house to pack up, our furniture and belongings were caked with river mud, and all manner of creatures crawled and slithered through the house, including a snake that dangled from one of the doorknobs. The cycle of flood and drought is a constant theme in the literature, art, and films of the northeast—and a sociological reality, as recurrent waves of migrants are forced to escape the arid *sertão*, or backlands, in search of food and employment in the city. This cyclical migration has caused overcrowding and extreme poverty in the city and its suburbs. I had the opportunity to make occasional forays into the *sertão* to visit friends at their ranches. This gave me a feeling for the landscape and people and was fundamental to my ability to render these details in the books I later translated.

New York City

I left Brazil in 1965 to attend Barnard College. The culture shock was intense. I had no knowledge of what American teenagers took for granted and was conspicuously out of step with pop culture, sports, dating customs, and the like. I did not then grasp (and have not since understood) American football, although I have a good idea of what is going on in a soccer game. I was a "third-culture kid," a term coined by the American sociologist Ruth Useem in the 1950s to describe the expatriate children who spend their formative years overseas. They are shaped by the multicultural environments and the worlds of their parents, who may work in international business, diplomacy, the military, the foreign service, church missions, and other jobs. The families relocate often and the children are educated in local and international schools, exposing them to peers who come from all over the world and who bond in a "third culture" that is world-spanning, diverse, empathic, and hard to understand by others who have not grown up this way. I identify with this group and have never lost the sense of being from everywhere and nowhere at the same time. There is the feeling that life is fleeting and mutable, that nothing is meant to last, and one takes refuge in the languages one speaks, in books, and in travel—a thirst never quenched. We are always on the outside looking in, collecting friends and experiences, yearning for stability yet rebelling against it. This life engenders a sense of existing in a state of becoming. Shapeshifting, summoning the best suited of the many identities within you to meet the place and moment you're in, becomes a survival skill that allows you to connect with anyone you meet. You rapidly identify the points of possible connection between yourself and the stranger, wherever they are from. Emily Wilson, Homer's most imaginative translator, says of herself, "I often feel like an Odysseus. He was always reinventing himself, and like a translator, pretending to be someone else, and telling that character's story. But maybe a true self can emerge from the lies" (Thurman 2023, 53). As third-culture kids, our own stories cannot be discerned from our appearance, our accent, or our belongings. We are trained to enter any situation with an open mind and heart, always ready to compromise and to trade in what we've picked up along the way, languages, insights, and mannerisms. Finally, we come to understand that belonging is not about place but about one's personal interests, ideas, and the people we have formed attachments to over time. One must follow one's inner compass and find grounding internally. Home exists only as an ideal: it is a place where the people you love see you for who you are.

I was thrilled to be in New York City and to be at a school then renowned for women's education—and for the opportunity not only to craft my own major in Latin American studies, the first one to do so at the college, but also to take classes "across the street" in Columbia's graduate program. There I was privileged to study with Charles Wagley, Ralph della Cava, Marvin Harris, Kempton Webb, and others who would transform interdisciplinary scholarship on Latin America. Kempton Webb's geography course and his book *The Changing Face of Northeast Brazil* (1974), published when I was in graduate school, helped me understand the region in a more nuanced light. Ralph della Cava's work on religion and society in Brazil, particularly messianism in the northeast, greatly influenced my interest in this topic in Brazilian literature and resonated when I retranslated Euclides da Cunha's iconic book *Os sertões* (1902; *Backlands: The Canudos Campaign*, 2010). Anthropologist Charles Wagley's pioneering work on race in Brazil, and particularly the Brazilian *caboclo*, deepened my understanding of the complexities of racial identities in Brazil and influenced my work in translating Darcy Ribeiro and Euclides da Cunha. Wagley left his position as director of the Latin American Institute at Columbia for a position as distinguished research professor at the University of Florida, where he spearheaded the development of the Center for Tropical Conservation and Development. I would later meet him and other Columbia professors again at the University of Florida when I joined the faculty in 1988. Gregory Rabassa, with whom I took courses in Latin American literature as an undergraduate, became my mentor and PhD supervisor at CUNY Graduate Center in the program he started (with funding from the Gulbenkian Foundation) in Lusophone literary studies and translation in the department of comparative literature.

I was particularly well suited to the experience of an urban campus and delighted in taking advantage of all the city had to offer. I got a part-time job at the then Bank of China (Taiwan) on Wall Street and was well treated by the bank manager, who liked to talk about literature. Occasionally on weekends and holidays, my roommates and I visited my aunt Mady in Woodstock, New York, where we hung out at the Espresso Café and even met and had coffee with the young and then unknown Bob Dylan, who played and sang there on weekends. My parents at the time were posted in Costa Rica, and we could only communicate by snail mail and the occasional phone call. Once I got in trouble with the Barnard dorm matron for staying out (with my first boyfriend) after the 11:00 pm curfew. To my chagrin and disbelief, the college patched a call through to my father via the US consulate in Recife, causing an "international incident," in my parents' words, and there was hell to pay! I spent summers with them in Recife, and—after they were transferred in my junior year—in San José, Costa Rica, where I learned guitar, went to a secretarial school to learn how to speed type (one of the most useful skills I've learned!), and volunteered at a local school.

This was a heady time in Morningside Heights. The unrest spreading through the country, which included the civil rights movement, the decline of urban centers in America, and opposition to the Vietnam War, came together with force at Columbia. In April 1968, I and more than a thousand other protesters took to the streets. Some occupied five buildings on the university campus until they were forced to leave by the police. This led to the retirement of President Grayson Kirk and the creation of the university senate, where faculty, alumni, and students gained a stronger voice in university matters. I met my first husband, Jonathan Lowe, in Kempton Webb's class, and we lived through these events together. Jon was getting his master's degree at the Columbia University School of International Affairs, with an area specialization in Latin American studies. He had been on a summer program in Peru in 1963 with the Experiment in International Living and spent his junior year abroad with New York University in Madrid. It was an intense courtship, I was deeply in love, and we got engaged in San José, Costa Rica, on a Christmas 1968 visit to my parents and siblings. We were married in Woodstock, New York, in June 1969, just before the famous festival (which occurred on a dairy farm in Bethel, New York) in August. By that time Jon was in basic training and I was working in New York City, still living in my student apartment. He had been drafted after we had successfully applied to the Peace Corps, wanting to get out of the country and away from the war, but the draft superseded the Peace Corps assignment. Seeking to avoid combat, Jon enlisted in Army Intelligence. He generously suggested that I go on to graduate school as planned—I had been accepted at Stanford for a master's program in Latin American studies—but I did not want to start our marriage with an indefinite separation, even though we were keenly aware of the uncertainty that military service posed. We spent six months in Baltimore, Maryland, where Jon attended the US Army Intelligence School at Fort Holabird, and I worked as an assistant to an architect and attended night classes in American literature at Johns Hopkins.

Germany Revisited

After six months at Fort Holabird, Jon was assigned to Munich, Germany. Our time in Germany was remarkably carefree, considering that Jon had narrowly escaped being drafted to Vietnam.; an officer friend had told Jon he was "on the list" to be assigned there. It was an opportunity to reconnect with my German roots. My former nanny, Clarissa, who had greeted me at the plane in Nuremberg on that freezing December day in 1947, was now working as a physician's assistant in obstetrics at the US Army hospital at McGraw Kaserne in Munich; it had been used by the US military during the occupation of Germany after World War II. During the 1970s, when we were there, it was the home of the 66th Military Intelligence Group, where Jon was assigned. By a strange "multiverse" coincidence, Jon also arrived in the middle of a freezing December night on a military transport plane, just as I had when I was a baby. I joined him a few months later. We lived "on the economy" in a studio apartment on Tegernseer Landstraße, next to the soccer stadium that is still there today. I worked at the US Army Education Center doing educational testing and college placement counseling for offboarding soldiers. I continued my education at the University of Munich (Ludwig-Maximilian-Universität), taking German language and culture classes that were accepted toward my entrance requirements at the CUNY Graduate Center. Jon and I took advantage of every opportunity to travel around Europe in our little red Ford Capri. We regularly enjoyed meals and outings with Clarissa and my father's old school friends who were still living in Munich, among them Fee von Reichlin, an actress who became prominent after World War II in the theaters and cabarets of Munich, and Bernd Scheublein, owner of the famed Paulaner Brewery. There were visits to Ohlstadt; skiing trips to the German, Austrian, and Swiss Alps; road trips to neighboring countries, including Holland in tulip season, when we stayed on a tulip farm; and even a long backpacking adventure to mainland Greece and the Greek isles. On February 10, 1970, I boarded a plane home to visit my parents (Jon remained in Munich, since he was on duty). The plane was taxiing on the runway when it suddenly stopped and turned around. The pilot announced that he had been ordered to abort the flight. We remained on the tarmac for eight hours. As things unfolded, we found out that three terrorists had attacked El-Al passengers on a bus at the Munich airport with guns and grenades. One passenger was killed and eleven were injured. All three terrorists were captured by airport police. The Action Organization for the Liberation of Palestine and the Popular Democratic Front for the Liberation of Palestine claimed responsibility for the attack. I recall watching the swarm of police and emergency vehicles from the plane window, hearing blaring sirens, and not knowing what to think. When we were finally allowed to disembark, I took a taxi home.

We left Munich when Jon ended his tour of duty in early 1972. Just six months later, during the 1972 Summer Olympics, eight members of the Palestinian militant organization Black September infiltrated the Olympic Village, killing two Israeli athletes and taking nine others as hostages. The resulting disaster, after the terrorists and hostages were flown by helicopter to Fürstenfeldbruck Air Base, is well known as a failure of planning and execution, in part because the postwar constitution forbade the better-trained German army to aid the civilian police. In the end, eleven Israelis were killed, along with one Munich policeman and five terrorists. Three gunmen were captured. Considering the continuing anguish of the Israeli-Palestinian conflict, as much as things change, they have remained the same.

Home Again To New York

When we returned to the United States, Jon started a lending officer training track program at Chase Bank International, and after two years he joined the Brazilian desk. I began my graduate studies at CUNY in 1973 in the comparative literature program under the direction of Gregory Rabassa. Justly considered one of the greatest translators in the English language, Rabassa brought his sense of humor, rugged discipline, and exquisite sensibility to languages to his classes. The next four years led me to discover my great passion in life, literary translation, and to my career in teaching and scholarship. Rabassa's wise and practical guidance kept me on track and focused on the goal. He reminded us that it was essential to finish the degree as soon as possible. An old soldier, proud of his service as an infantryman and cryptographer during World War II, he compared earning the PhD to earning our "stripes." Get the job done and go on to do the work, he would say. Rabassa had always maintained that a good translator had to be a good writer. Being a trained linguist was not enough. Bringing a text into one language from another, as the German word *übersetzen* implies, is not literary translation; turning a text into literature that reproduces the original is another thing entirely. The other requisite for the translator is to be well-read and to know how to read. From deep reading and careful listening comes a multilayered appreciation for the infinite possibilities of language and inter-language work. Rabassa would hold forth in the bar at the top floor of the Graduate Center after our early evening classes and regale us with his jokes, puns (the more multilingual the better), stories that he embellished each time he told them, and bawdy limericks.

During my studies I met and worked with fellow students and professors who would become lifelong collaborators and friends. Burton Pike, with whom I had taken classes and who was on my dissertation committee, impressed me with his kindness and eagerness to work with students whose specialties were geographically far afield from his own expertise in German and French literature. A master translator himself, he had a strong research interest in the city in literature, which became my focus. I formed fast friendships with a few fellow students. Earl Fitz shared my excitement about Clarice Lispector, and we later did the first translation of her *Água viva* (1973; *The*

Stream of Life, 1988). We coauthored *Translation and the Rise of Inter-American Literature* (2007), a project that combined our academic interests and our conviction about the agency of the translator. Adelaide (April) Monteiro Batista, from the Azores, became a close friend. She and I studied and roomed together in the summer of 1973 at the University of Coimbra, taking train trips to visit her relatives on weekends. Back at our studies in New York, we drove from New York City to visit her family in New Bedford, Massachusetts. Monika Forndran, who was pursuing the comparative literature degree with specializations in French and German, would later earn a degree in copyright law and become the godmother of our son Alan. Patricia Wallace Costa was earning her PhD in comparative literature with a focus on French and Italian. I was able to help facilitate the adoption of her son Daniele in Bogotá years later. She eventually moved to Brussels with her Italian husband, Antonio Costa, who had a distinguished career at the United Nations while she pursued her academic career at Vesalius University.

I worked as a research assistant and then as a graduate assistant teaching Portuguese at Queens College. I loved the stimulation of the ideas and projects that flowed through the Graduate Center and took part in as many of the extra activities as I could. Jon and I moved into a one-bedroom apartment at 20 East Ninth Street in Greenwich Village, a block away from NYU, where I now teach in the master's program in translation and interpreting. When I was newly pregnant with Alicia (and very proud that I was to become a mother), I traveled to Brazil on an OAS fellowship in 1976 that allowed me to spend three months doing research on my dissertation. I had to "hide" my pregnancy from the program administrators (I believe that at that time, we were not supposed to be on the program while expecting); they commented every time I checked in that I must be enjoying the Brazilian food. During that time, I traveled throughout Brazil, interviewing the writers I was translating. That work would become the focus of my dissertation and later book, *The City in Brazilian Literature* (1982). I spent a good amount of time with Clarice Lispector, visiting her Leme apartment for coffee and conversation and going to restaurants or to gatherings at the homes of Rubem Fonseca, Nélida Piñon, and others in their circle. The conversation was heady and important: all of them were in their prime, and they were politically engaged in the resistance against the dictatorship. Lispector would rub my pregnant belly and, in her sonorous voice, declare that the baby was a girl. She gave me a soapstone duck off her bookshelf for the baby. (It still has a place of honor on my own bookshelf.) Her little dog Ulysses would perform tricks for us as we sipped our *cafezinhos* in her living room, surrounded by paintings of the stunningly beautiful Lispector at different stages of her life.

Alicia (Spanish pronunciation *uh-LIS-ee-uh*—in typical expatriate fashion, it never occurred to me at the time that it would be pronounced any other way) was named after my paternal grandmother, whose English name, Alice, was fashionable in Germany in 1888, when she was born. Alicia arrived nine hours after I put the last period on my dissertation. I felt a sudden rush of tiredness and went into our bedroom to take a nap. That is when my water broke. I called the doctor, who directed me to go to the hospital. I phoned Jon at work and asked him to take the dissertation, packed up in a ream-sized box stuffed with my typewritten manuscript, to the CUNY Graduate Center and then join me at Lenox Hill Hospital. It was a bumpy taxi ride to the hospital on that beautiful April day, the panic-stricken cabbie passing tulips in bloom along Park Avenue. Jon made it in plenty of time, and Alicia was safely delivered in the wee hours of the morning, to our boundless joy. Rubem and Thea Fonseca, her godparents, traveled from Rio for her christening at Grace Church in the Village.

Leaving New York: Colombia to Florida

When Alicia was three months old, we moved to Bogotá, Colombia. Jon was assigned by Chase to their Chase Regional Representative Office, where he had business development responsibilities with, over time, all the Andean countries as well as Paraguay and Uruguay. I had a Fulbright grant that provided a teaching position at the Universidad Javeriana and allowed me to travel around the country to lecture at different regional universities and cultural centers. We remained in Colombia until 1982. It was a tumultuous time in the country's history of guerrilla warfare, kidnappings, labor strikes, and general unrest, which had its roots in the conflict known as La Violencia, itself set off by the 1948 murder of liberal political leader Jorge Eliécer Gaitán. The anti-Communist repression in Colombia in the 1960s led Liberal and Communist militants to reorganize into the Revolutionary Armed Forces of Colombia (FARC). The "Colombian conflict" that began in May 1964, a systematic series of wars between the government, far-right paramilitary groups, crime syndicates, and leftist guerrilla groups, continued into the 1970s and early 1980s. According to Colombia's National Center for Historical Memory, more than two hundred thousand people died between 1958 and 2013—many of them civilians—and more than five million civilians had to leave their homes. While security was a concern, and the Chase security team added burglar bars to our rented townhome, our lives were relatively free. We enjoyed immersing ourselves in Colombian culture and traveling around the country. I taught all my university classes in Spanish, which forced me to bring my proficiency up to a professional level. I grew in appreciation for the beauty and precision of spoken and written Colombian Spanish, the work of Colombian writers, and the country's strong literary tradition as well as the academic rigor of my Jesuit priest colleagues at the Javeriana. They exemplified the educational philosophy of the Jesuit tradition, which approaches academic subjects holistically, exploring the connections among facts, insights, conclusions, problems, and solutions. One of the oldest universities in Latin America, the Javeriana was founded by the Society of Jesus in 1623 and has traditionally educated the Colombian elite. It was the first higher education institution in Colombia to be awarded institutional accreditation by the Colombian Ministry of Education. It is a comprehensive research university with 18 schools, 61 departments, and 242 academic programs. My colleagues, among them rising Colombian writers whose work I began to translate, included us in social activities. I formed productive relationships with Eduardo Márceles Daconte, Rodrigo Parra, Jorge Eliécer Pardo, Montserrat Ordóñez, Sarah de Mojica, and others, eventually publishing translations in literary magazines and writing about the authors for scholarly journals. In collaboration with the Brazilian consulate in Bogotá and the Universidad Javeriana, I organized a special festival of Brazilian literature, though it had to be postponed because of the kidnapping of the American ambassador Diego Asencio. On February 27, 1980, M-19 terrorists broke into a diplomatic reception at the Dominican Republic's embassy in Bogotá, took many hostages (including fourteen ambassadors) at gunpoint, and demanded the freedom of 311 prisoners and $50 million in cash. Diego Asencio, whom we later met and worked with at the University of Florida, played a key role in the negotiations, and after sixty-one days the hostages were released unharmed. The kidnappers got no prisoners and a $2.5 million ransom. Fidel Castro offered sanctuary to the guerrillas and protection for the hostages. Diego and his wife, Nancy, wrote a book about the experience titled *Our Man Is Inside* (1983).

During our time in Colombia, we experienced protests, political violence, labor strikes, and earthquakes. Some quakes were quite severe, over seven degrees of magnitude on the Richter scale. We also enjoyed the country's natural beauty and its cultural traditions. We traveled around the country as a family and visited neighboring countries in the Andean region. I traveled with Jon numerous times to all the Andean countries as well as to Argentina. For me the most unforgettable trip was the one we made from Argentina to Chile over the pristine lakes. A close second was a trip to southern Chile, sailing through the Chilean fjords, and there was also a sailing exploration of the Galapagos. Little Alicia attended Winnie the Pooh Nursery School and then the international school, Colegio Nueva Granada. She became bilingual in Spanish and English. Her safety was a constant concern, and I experienced a moment of blind panic when she failed to appear at the bus stop after school. She walked home and appeared after a short while, saying that she had gotten off at the wrong stop, but the shock was long lasting. Life in Bogotá was intense, personally and professionally, and the connections and work we did there yielded fruit in the years to follow.

When Jon's tour of duty was up with Chase, we made the decision to try to get a posting in Florida. Given its multiculturalism, its ties to Latin America, and its role as an international business hub, it seemed like a good choice for us, after so many years living as expatriates. Jon had been offered a post as country manager of the Dominican Republic, but we turned it down because we agreed that it was time to get back to the United States, which could afford me professional development opportunities. The 1980s were iconic years in Miami. The natural color and vitality of the city were accentuated by drug wars, waves of immigration, and a business boom. The city was going through a cultural revolution, and the lush atmosphere created a vibrant mix of fashion, parties, loud music, and art. It was an architectural golden age, too, when architects introduced modern buildings typified by abstract designs in bold colors and graphics that transformed the Miami skyline and South Beach. The languages spoken on the street were a dizzying mix of Spanglish, Creole, Portuguese, and Caribbean dialects. After settling into our home in Kendall, I took a job first at Florida International University, working in international programs, and then with Miami-Dade Community College (later renamed Miami-Dade College) in the foreign languages department and as head of international programs. My father moved to Miami to live near us shortly after my mother died in 1984. He had suffered a stroke and had difficulty walking and using his right arm and hand. I helped him pack up his home in Woodstock, New York, and we then took the auto train to Sanford, Florida, and drove to Miami. After living with us for several months, Dad moved to an assisted-living facility near Baptist Hospital, the "Sunrise Club," where he lived happily until Hurricane Andrew wiped out Miami in 1992 and literally knocked the breath out of him. Miami infrastructure had been destroyed and the electricity was out for days. I had found an aide for my father through an agency, and she attended him faithfully; after the hurricane it took several days for her to be able to visit my father, and not even the staff of the facility could give immediate help to the residents. Just four months after the storm, my father died in Baptist Hospital after a short illness. Jamaican-born Hyacinth took care of my father for several years and even traveled with him to Europe. My father took great pride in introducing her to his German friends, who were fascinated by her Caribbean beauty. She became a member of the family, and we are still close, all these years later. We call each other "sister" and continue to visit and call each other regularly.

My marriage to Jon dissolved in 1987, a wrenching life change made on my initiative. I attribute it in part to the trauma of my diagnosis and treatment for breast cancer in 1984, shortly after my mother's death from the disease, and to my own ever-seeking, restless, third-culture personality. Jon's continual long hours at work and incessant travel had affected our relationship, too, especially toward the end of the Bogotá assignment, at which time one of the biggest financial crises was developing in Latin America. We had found out that I was pregnant shortly before my diagnosis (after miscarriages in Colombia, where the altitude had negative effects on my health), and the very new pregnancy had to be terminated during the mastectomy surgery. The shock and depression that overtook our lives led me to think that I could "edit" my life by taking it in a new direction, although of course it doesn't work that way. After struggling with remorse for many years, I am now at peace with my past. This is largely a result of the grace of forgiveness from Jon as well as Alicia, who is one of the kindest, most capable, and emotionally intelligent women I know.

To North Central Florida And Beyond

I did learn that blessings come in surprising ways and in many forms, despite ourselves. After a rough period of transition, I moved with Alicia and son Alan, whom Jon and I had adopted after my breast cancer treatments, to Gainesville, Florida, to join a colleague, political scientist Terry McCoy. Terry and I had been working together on establishing the Florida/Brazil Institute, an initiative started by Governor Bob Graham as a community college–university partnership designed to foster educational and cultural ties between Florida and Brazil, the state's largest trading partner. I was the Miami-Dade College faculty representative, and he was the University of Florida's designated director of the initiative. We had formed a close personal bond and had fallen in love in Rio (a different kind of love than my first love, and at another time and place). We married in 1988. Terry was born and raised in Ohio, and to me, the Midwest was a foreign country that I was curious to visit. He took me on a road trip through Ohio and the upper Midwest, the first of many visits to family and friends. I enjoy hearing the accents and speech cadences of Midwesterners (Terry has a distinct twang and places stress on syllables in a way that seems odd to me, something we joke about), the rolling hills and fall colors of Ohio, the majesty of the Great Lakes, and the excitement of its big cities. It has been a rich marriage that I would describe as a lively, ongoing conversation accentuated by travel adventures and the joy of sailing. I am grateful that Jon and I rebuilt a loving relationship and continued to raise our children together until they reached adulthood. Terry, in turn, has been a supportive, caring stepfather, and he and Jon are friendly, so we became a diverse and entertaining blended family that includes Terry's two older children, Julie and Dan, who were already launched into the world at the time we married (and of whom I am deeply fond); six grandchildren who give us great joy; and our respective extended families of siblings and their offspring. My father would jokingly call me "Dona Flor" (referring to Amado's *Dona Flor e seus dois maridos*) when we gathered, quite often, for family meals with both husbands present. We bonded over family crises, clinging to each other when Alicia was on the scene across the street from the World Trade Center when the 9/11 terror attacks began. She had just left the PATH subway and gone into her office across the street when the planes hit. We lost contact for a few hours, and when she called in safe after making her way on foot to the Hoboken ferry, through the ash and horror of that morning, we breathed a collective sigh of gratitude.

Gainesville was a good place to bring up children, given the ease of movement around the city and the good medical and educational services. Alicia attended public schools, excelling in sports and theater, and Alan received excellent care for his Asperger's condition, even though it was not well recognized, diagnosed, or understood at the time. Dr. Ann Alexander, founder of The Morris Center in Gainesville, was a groundbreaking developmental pediatrician who treated him from the time he was three for symptoms including speech delay shortly after we relocated. She did not diagnose the autism spectrum per se but did focus on early, life-changing interventions. Eventually Alan was diagnosed at age fourteen with pervasive developmental disorder, a diagnosis that was refined in subsequent evaluations as Asperger's. Today Alan is a high-functioning adult who manages his Asperger's wisely.

We enjoyed sailing as a couple and as a family on our Hunter 34 sloop, *The Real McCoy*. We berthed it first in St. Augustine's Camachee Cove Marina and then, after sailing it around Florida in 1991, at the Harborage in St. Petersburg, where the children could more easily visit their father on weekends. We upgraded to a C&C 38, the *Dona Flor*, and took Alicia and Alan on cruises to Key West and to the Dry Tortugas. In 2003 we acquired a brand-new thirty-four-foot Beneteau, the *Sweet Leilani* (my childhood nickname is Lani, bestowed on me by my father because of his romantic fascination with Hawaii), that we picked up in Bradenton, Florida, kept at the Harborage Marina in St. Petersburg for three years, and then sailed back around Florida to St. Augustine, where we again held a slip in Camachee Cove. Sadly, our sailing days have come to an end, and our beloved Beneteau was recently sold. The new owners trucked it down I-75 to its new home in St. Petersburg. The plan is to continue to find ways to spend time on and near the water.

Terry and I traveled often to Latin America for university work and on United States Information Agency (USIA) lecture tours. This gave me the opportunity to return to Brazil many times and to keep current with my literary contacts and translation projects. Together we met and hosted heads of state, university presidents, writers, artists, and colleagues all over Latin

America. We were invited to attend Luiz Inácio Lula da Silva's visit to the office of the chair of the Senate Foreign Relations Committee in Washington on one of his presidential campaigns, and we later encountered then representative Lula in the halls of the Brazilian Congress. We visited Jorge Amado and Zélia Gattai at their home in Salvador for a lively afternoon of conversation with members of Salvador's literature and art community. We attended dinners and soirees at the homes of writers and artists all over Brazil. The vice president of Ecuador dined at our home, escorted by his smartly uniformed security detail. The guards stood at attention at our front door, to Alan's fascination and delight.

On a USIA-sponsored trip to Guyana in 1991, we met with then opposition leader Cheddi Jagan, who had been kept out of office by the United States because of his left-wing politics. The visit, on which we were both USIA scholars, was part of a change in US policy. Mr. Jagan engaged Terry in a question-and-answer session after Terry's talk in Guyana and publicly thanked him for his contribution to democratic dialogue in his country. Terry and I later hosted Jagan and his wife after he became president—with a full secret service entourage—on a visit to the University of Florida.

On the same USIA trip, we traveled in a propeller plane over a dense jungle to neighboring Suriname, where our lecture program was also a US government effort to support democracy. At a luncheon at the home of the US ambassador to Suriname, we were seated next to Desiré Delano Bouterse, who was then head of the National Military Council and who, from that position, ruled the country like a dictator. Terry was appointed to talk with him about the role of public opinion in democratic government. We did this with Bouterse's security guards standing around the room—at ease, but with weapons on display. During the 2010 presidential elections, Bouterse was elected president. In 2019 he was convicted by a Surinamese court for the murder of fifteen opponents in 1982 following a coup to seize power; the man who had dominated the former Dutch colony's recent history was sentenced to twenty years in prison. Bouterse subsequently disappeared and never served his sentence. (He is rumored to be living in hiding in Brazil.)

Gainesville, about seventy miles southwest of Jacksonville, is a university town that has grown up around the state's flagship institution of higher learning, the University of Florida (UF). Once a Timucuan village, the land where the city is situated became part of a Spanish land grant to Don Fernando de la Maza Arredondo, a Spanish merchant, in 1817. In 1824, after Florida was annexed to the United States, Alachua County was created, and the population grew with an influx of planters and farmers when Florida won statehood in 1845. During the Civil War, the town was the site of a Confederate storehouse. After the war, education started to become the town's most important economic driver. UF had its beginnings in 1853, when Governor Thomas Brown signed a bill supporting higher education in the state. The East Florida Seminary was the first of these state-supported institutions, and in 1866 it relocated from Ocala to Gainesville. The second precursor to UF was the Florida Agricultural College, established in Lake City in 1884. It became the state's first land-grant college. In 1903, the Florida legislature changed the name to the University of Florida. The Buckman Act of 1905 restructured Florida's higher education system. Six state-supported institutions were combined and reorganized into three schools segregated by race and gender. These eventually became Florida State University and Florida A&M University. Gainesville was chosen for the University of Florida, and campus construction began in 1905. The school started accepting some white women students in 1932 and became fully coeducational after World War II. It was racially integrated in 1958. Now it has an enrollment of more than sixty thousand and was recently ranked fifth nationally among public universities in the United States.

When I arrived at UF in 1988, the Center for Latin American Studies had achieved national and international prominence. Terry, who specialized in Latin American politics and the business environment, was the director. The Center had been founded in 1930, under the name Institute for Inter-American Affairs, by then president John J. Tigert. It was the first research center in the United States to focus on Latin America. Tigert had served as the first US commissioner of education (1922–28) and was aware of the growing importance of foreign affairs at a national level, seeking to promote the "Good Neighbor Policy" of the Hoover and Roosevelt administrations. Interest in Latin America at UF is also the natural result of Florida's geographical and political role in US–Latin American relations, its Spanish heritage, and its large Spanish-speaking population. The Institute's inaugural conference was held in 1931 among the events marking the university's twenty-fifth anniversary. As part of the closing ceremony, UF Plaza of the Americas was dedicated with twenty-one live oaks, one for each of the American republics at the time. The university began to recruit students from Latin America, strengthened its Latin American curriculum, and developed agreements with Latin American universities. The Master of Arts in Latin American Studies has been offered since 1952. In 1962, the Institute was awarded Title VI funding and has continuously received funds to support its programs. In 1963, it was renamed the Center for Latin American Studies, and its growing faculty has had a leadership role in the development of the field nationally and internationally. The *Handbook of Latin American Studies*, the premier bibliography on the region, was published between 1949 and 1978 by the University of Florida Press, which has continued to publish titles of importance to the field in a variety of disciplines, including literature and translation.

When I started my work at UF, there was an initiative underway to promote and expand its international mission. After a year teaching in the Romance languages and literatures department, I was appointed by President John Lombardi, a Latin American historian, to establish a new International Center along with a colleague, the late Dr. Richard Downie. I also continued in my role as codirector of the Florida/Brazil Institute, now in collaboration with a colleague at my previous academic home, Miami-Dade College. Together we began the task of collecting information on the huge array of international initiatives at the university, seeking new funding opportunities for international programs, and strengthening university-wide study-abroad options. The International Center has had a series of directors, and I worked under several of them, including Dr. Uma Lele, a World Bank agricultural economist whose connections with the Carter Center led to personal contact with Jimmy Carter and my involvement as program coordinator (on UF's behalf) in his Global Development Initiative. This project took our research and development team to Israel, Jordan, and the West Bank, where we conducted a community development and peacekeeping initiative designed to foster collaboration and good relations between bordering towns in the West Bank and Israel around a wetlands park project. I had the opportunity to meet in person with Yasser Arafat on one of the visits to give him and his advisers a courtesy briefing on the Carter project. As "chief of party" on our Carter Foundation–sponsored grant, I was selected to speak directly to Arafat, who gallantly gave me a kiss on the cheek after our conversation. It was our hope and goal to make a small contribution to Israeli-Arab peace initiatives. My efforts to seek funding for a wide variety of International Center–based projects were rewarded with a major grant from the Lucent Foundation in 1999 to develop online learning programs that would strengthen our ties with universities in Latin America. This opened the door to an associate director position in the Center for Latin American Studies under the new director, Charles Wood, who succeeded Terry. I continued my work in program development and, at Charles's suggestion, started a program in translation studies under the auspices of the Center. Charles shared my vision of translation as a key curriculum offering in a university with an international mission—and a natural fit for its multilingual student population. Establishing the program turned into one of my most rewarding, if challenging, tasks. At the time, the language departments were not keen on such a program, perhaps because some faculty still failed to recognize translation studies as an academic discipline, and some apparently considered it a threat to their own enrollments and autonomy. Even though we consulted widely and sought collaboration from the departments, the project ultimately remained within the Center. I developed the language-neutral curriculum (students who worked in any language pair were accepted) and aligned it with American Translators Association certification standards. Soon we were attracting students from all over campus and the community, from a diverse array of languages and cultural backgrounds, who greeted the program with enthusiasm. I was fortunate to draw in talented colleagues to teach in the program, including Tom Ratican, a former National Security Agency linguist, and Bernadette Cesar-Lee, a Belgian-trained professional translator and adjunct faculty member in the Romance languages and literatures department. Dr. Janet Gomez, presently at New York University, was my brilliant student assistant at the time. She helped me set up and monitor the terminology and Computer Assisted Technologies lab at UF, a first for the university. During my twenty years at UF, I continued my active translation practice and critical writing on translation, working with authors as diverse as Machado de Assis, Darcy Ribeiro, and the contemporary Brazilian writers I had been associated with since my graduate student days. I formed a productive relationship with the University Press of Florida, which published my second book (written with Earl Fitz), *Translation and the Rise of Inter-American Literature* (2007), and Darcy Ribeiro's *O povo brasileiro* (1995; *The Brazilian People*, 2000). To our delight, Gregory Rabassa responded positively to my request that he translate the Ribeiro book, one of the foundational works of the famous sociologist and statesman. I wrote the introduction. I made connections with faculty on campus who had an interest in translation or were practicing literary translators. I helped organize the 1991 American Literary Translators Association conference in collaboration with the late Harold H. Hanson, who founded the translation journal *Delos* with a grant from the Ford Foundation.

While at the Center for Latin American Studies, I also had the opportunity to work with the late linguist Dr. Martha J. (M. J.) Hardman on a National Science Foundation project to document the endangered Jaqi languages of Peru and Bolivia. M. J. and her Peruvian husband, the late Dimas Bautista Iturrizaga, were pioneers in anthropological linguistics. She met her husband in Tupe, Peru, while studying the Indigenous languages there, and her work resulted in the first written grammar for the Jaqaru language in Peru. The NSF grant that we received, for which she and I served as co-principal investigators, enabled the digitization of the Jaqi languages (Jaqaru, Kawki, and Aymara) and made me aware of the importance of translation expertise for the documentation of endangered languages. The translator's insights and strategies can assist with rendering concepts that have no exact equivalent, and with the help of bridge translations into major languages, the worldview and experiences of the Jaqi-speaking peoples can be preserved. The grant took us on an extensive field trip to Peru and Bolivia, where we recorded and photographed some of the last speakers of the language. Back on the UF campus, we worked with an interdisciplinary team to design and populate the trilingual (Aymara, Jaqaru, and English) website with language data that included the texts themselves, accompanying photographs, cultural notes, and (uniquely) a complete annotation of the grammatical structure of the texts. Word and morpheme dictionaries with concordances are generated by the site. The goal was to make the resource available to heritage speakers and for linguistic research. Since that effort, groups of volunteers have translated Facebook into Aymara as part of the language-preservation efforts. The group translated more than twenty-four thousand words into Aymara, the number Facebook requires before launching the site in a new language (BBC News 2015).

A Move to Illinois

My until then eclectic career took a sharp turn toward a focus on translation in 2008, when I was offered the position of founding director of the Center for Translation Studies at the University of Illinois at Urbana-Champaign (UIUC). I was thrilled with the opportunity to build a master's program in translation studies from the ground up, a program that would be delivered both on campus and online. Around the time that this opportunity arose, the University of Florida had started to shrink its language programs, gutting some entirely, and there had been a change in leadership at the Center for Latin American Studies that was less supportive of the translation program I had created. I took this as the right moment to make a change, and while the move presented numerous challenges, personal and professional, it was undoubtedly the right thing to do. Terry was offered a position with the UIUC College of Business, teaching a Latin American Business Environment course and leading a yearly study-abroad trip to Brazil. An added bonus was that Alicia and her family were now living in Ohio, a mere six hours' drive away—much closer than Florida! I felt that I had finally found an academic home in the School of Literatures, Cultures, and Linguistics, then headed by Dr. Doug Kibbee, who had hired me. He was a believer in the central role of translation in the humanities, and he tirelessly lobbied and prodded his colleagues and the university administrators to elevate translation studies in the university's curriculum. Kibbee, a linguist, specializes in the history of the French language, language policy, and translation. His work on translations of *Alice in Wonderland* has taken him on lecture tours around the world. His mentoring, kindness, hospitality, and support were crucial to my getting my feet on the ground at UIUC. In addition to his academic prowess, Doug is a master baker, and he greeted me on my first day with freshly baked baguettes on my office table.

The UIUC School of Literatures, Cultures, and Linguistics was a suitable location for the new Center for Translation Studies, given its internationally recognized research and teaching that focuses on the analysis of culture, broadly understood. It is also a center for cutting-edge language-related research and pedagogy as well as for linguistic expertise across many languages. As an incubator for a new master's degree in translation and interpreting, it provided human and material resources critical for the development of the program. My mission was to create an interdisciplinary, multilingual translation program that would attract students from across the school and across campus and prepare them for work in a variety of language-related careers and professional pathways. This involved intensive consultation with university faculty and administrators as well as networking with professional organizations and other master's programs in translation and interpreting in the United States, Europe, China, and South America. My vision was to create two parallel programs, one on campus and the other entirely online. The online program required support and collaboration with the university's online-learning division.

Another important reason for the university's interest in creating the program was the active presence of Dalkey Archive Press on campus, directed and founded by the late John O'Brien. Our goal was to develop an educational partnership that would provide internship opportunities allowing translation students to gain experience in translation publishing. It was our experience that many literary translation students have only a vague idea of the publishing process and the importance of understanding how it works and what their role might be. The program was designed for translators at an early stage in their careers who would benefit from working closely with an editor and learning about the many aspects of translation-focused publishing. The internship dovetailed with the MA course in literary translation, which focused not just on the fundamentals of literary translation but also on how to approach agents and publishers, how to write a sample translation and a proposal, and how to negotiate contracts. One important aspect of this training was teaching students how to assess the marketability of a literary work, which requires a sense for cultural gaps and how they might be bridged.

As a first step, I formed an advisory committee comprising faculty and administrators in all the school's departments and started the process of writing the curriculum for the master's degree. The curriculum had to be approved at various levels, starting with the school, the university senate, and finally the state board of education. During that process, I was called upon to explain the field of study, its interdisciplinary nature, its history, and its importance to the humanities. Many colleagues outside the discipline and the school wanted a clear justification for why the master's program was needed and what it would contribute to the school. I spent many hours of meetings explaining that translation studies had become a large interdisciplinary field encompassing the arts, humanities, social sciences, and computational linguistics. Important subfields include translation theory and literary translation, translation history, linguistic approaches to translation studies, special domain translation, machine translation, localization and transcreation, and interpreting studies. New work is emerging in the field of cognitive translation studies as well as on translation in education. Research on translation theory has progressed exponentially to include new areas of inquiry such as gender and race in translation, ethics, new media, foreignizing translation practice, linguistic hybridity, and the impact of colonialism and power politics on translation theory and practice. Edwin Gentzler, the American Germanist scholar, suggested in his book *Contemporary Translation Theories* (2001) that the future of translation studies is rich in possibilities and that a variety of academic and sociopolitical events occurring internationally have made conditions "ripe" for a translation turn in several fields simultaneously. Translation has enjoyed a renaissance in many countries and regions. Gentzler remarks, "I suggest that we are just scratching the surface and that in the coming years more studies from a variety of perspectives, cultures, and languages will emerge" (197).

I was keen to align the program with professional standards, including those of the International Standards Organization, the European Union Master of Translation consortium, and the American Translators Association, as well as the curriculum of established programs such as the Monterey (now Middlebury) Institute of International Studies, Kent State University, the University of Vienna's Zentrum für Translationswissenschaft, Université Paris-Diderot (Paris VII), Belgium's Center for Translation Studies at KU Leuven, Guangdong University in China, the Department of Foreign Languages at Tsinghua University, the School of Foreign Languages at Shanghai Jiao Tong University, and the Universidade Federal de Santa Catarina in Florianópolis, Brazil. We built partnerships with several of these universities and exchanged faculty. Jointly with our partners, we organized several international conferences on new topics and paradigms in translation studies; in collaboration with the university libraries, we hosted many writers and scholars for talks and events. In 2013, we received a National Endowment for the Humanities Summer Institute grant to support a two-week program for university and college faculty interested in expanding their curricular offerings to include translation and adding translation as a focus of personal scholarship and practice.

In designing the curriculum for the new University of Illinois program, it was clear to me that a multilingual rather than language-pair approach made sense both pedagogically and for program growth. Because of the fledgling program's small size and interdisciplinary orientation, it was not feasible to organize the curriculum around language pairs, although language-pair classes were available. The pedagogical approach to teaching in this modality required considerable thought and care. The focus was directed toward the student as the resident classroom language specialist. Students would be encouraged to do independent research and learning and then share their language and translation examples around specific translation problems with the class. The student-centered approach has its advantages: students acquire techniques for finding materials on their own, using instructor prompts. They also gain confidence and skill in locating and utilizing tools and resources they need to succeed in the professional translation environment. They become practiced in explaining their translation problems and solutions to their peers, as they will have to do for future clients throughout their careers. The learning process becomes an apprenticeship through guided independent learning, in which the instructor is focused on managing classroom work and evaluating the students' progress. This approach works with cognitive processing, involving interpreting and negotiating meaning in and out of the classroom.

Other areas that demanded curricular attention were translation for new media, translation and new technologies, new approaches to literary translation, and stylistics. The rapid evolution of translation technologies and the rise of digital humanities have created pressure for programs not only to include computer-assisted translation, machine translation, and a variety of software skills into the curriculum but also to teach students how to interface with digital texts and media. Rising translators today must have a wide range of skills outside the traditional subject mastery of special domain fields and language-pair skills. They must master software skills applicable to project management, terminology management, localization, and corpus analysis. And now they must also understand the concepts and use of artificial intelligence—all without forgetting that the foundation of translation work is the word. The fundamental skills for the translator are still reading, writing, editing, and researching.

Designing a program for online delivery required aligning new translation pedagogy with instructional design principles applicable to online learning. The guiding principle is the learner-centered virtual classroom, in which the instructor facilitates, provides intensive feedback, and encourages students to participate in a cohort-based learning community. It simulates real-world practice, where translators work primarily online with clients and colleagues. The online classroom encourages independent thinking, time management, the development of sophisticated Internet research skills, and good communication practices. Most of the work is done asynchronously, with the option for synchronous meetings with instructors or small groups on Zoom. In the early years of developing the University of Illinois online master's degree program, we had to learn how to teach not only traditional courses such as Theory and Practice of Translation but also subjects like terminology, computer-assisted translation and localization, and interpreting by using a variety of multimedia tools available on learning management system platforms such as Canvas, Blackboard, Moodle, and Brightspace. Integrating online library resources into our courses became a priority, and it was with the help of dedicated librarians like Paula Carns at the UIUC library that we began to increase and update holdings in translation and translation studies.

A Return to Florida

After seven years commuting between Illinois and Florida, I felt it was time to wrap up my work at UIUC. We graduated our first master's class in 2015, and with that mission accomplished, I decided to return to the south. I was longing to get back to sailing on the *Sweet Leilani* and to designing and tending to my Florida garden. Alan had benefited from our time in Illinois. He had been accepted as a client at the Developmental Services Center in Champaign, a nonprofit organization that supports the autism community. The staff assisted him with a variety of services, including community integration, independent living, and job placement. Their unstinting commitment to Alan made all the difference in his transition to independent adulthood. He has completed a degree in computer science, with a specialization in cybersecurity, at Santa Fe College in Gainesville.

My professional focus would continue to be on my literary translation work and online teaching. I was offered a position on the faculty of the New York University Master's in Translation and Interpreting, which I began in the fall of 2015. Along with my teaching, I did curriculum development for the program and helped move it toward the language-neutral, multilingual format that we had pioneered at UIUC. I was excited to be associated with NYU and my "hometown" of New York City. Although the work is online, I find reasons to travel to New York for events and meetings with colleagues and students. From 2016 to 2019, I taught summer translation workshops at Kenyon College with my colleague Katherine M. (Kate) Hedeen, who worked tirelessly with me to promote literary translation as an equal partner to the well-known creative writing workshops that the college has held for many years. I have also been active with the PEN America translation committee, serving twice as a juror for the PEN Literary Translation Award and working with the Manifesto Committee to draft the 2023 PEN America manifesto on literary translation. I received an NEA Literary Translation grant in 2020 for the translation of Nélida Piñon's early erotic novel, *A casa da paixão*, along with selected stories. I also received a Fulbright Scholar award to return to the Federal University of Santa Catarina in 2021, but the Covid-19 lockdown postponed (and eventually led me to cancel) that opportunity.

In an unexpected bit of serendipity, in 2022 I was invited to spend the spring semester at UMass Dartmouth through the Hélio and Amelia Pedroso Luso-American Development Foundation (FLAD) Endowed Chair of Portuguese Studies program sponsored by the Center for Portuguese Studies and Culture. The Center also houses Tagus Press, which has published three of my translations. I was beyond excited to teach the doctoral seminar Brazilian Literature in the Digital Age—my area of current interest—and to work with Mario Pereira at Tagus on new translation proposals. I also led an informal translation workshop for students and the community. The time there was enriching and productive and offered the luxury of space for quiet contemplation and study. The energy and dedication of my students fed my imagination and gratified my soul. Their enthusiasm for the seminar topic was not only affirming but motivating; I felt encouraged to continue to pursue that line of research. After two years of teaching exclusively online owing to the pandemic, it was a joy to return to the physical classroom. The Center for Portuguese Studies and Culture generously sponsored three of the writers we were studying to join us on campus for a colloquium on social movements and civic engagement in the Lusophone world. Paulo Dutra, J. P. Cuenca, and Noemi Jaffe participated in the two-day event and met with students during their stay. I enjoyed exploring the culture and life of that ruggedly beautiful corner of New England, the center of Portuguese and Azorean immigration in the United States. Hearing Portuguese spoken on the streets, meeting third-generation Portuguese with surnames from the Lusophone world, and reading signage in Portuguese made me smile. The time passed by all too quickly.

Now that I am back in Gainesville, I am moved to gather my thoughts about translation, my journey to becoming a translator, what I have learned from teaching translation, the pleasures and perils of the profession, and the issues that are transforming the practice and that we must account for in today's world. This book is but one of several such memoirs. Like translation itself, which invites many readings and renderings of a work, each translator's unique story adds to the knowledge that we gain from the process, the practice, and the product of the craft.

Translation in Other Words

When Edie published her book Why Translation Matters with Yale, I remember talking with her about why, of all the interpretive arts, translation had to defend itself against the insensitive and damaging charges of whether it was even possible to do so. Or not traitorous. No one asks a pianist or a dancer or an actor such a question. We depend on literary translators to illuminate a work and bring it to us. We depend on the rigorous efforts that were made to prepare the interpretation and the delight in performing them. We appreciate the love that was expressed throughout.

John Donatich, "A Tribute to Edith Grossman," September 6, 2023

Reading, Hearing the Text, and Following the Words

Translation begins with close reading. This is the core of our practice, and we are compelled to read and dissect each word and sentence of our source text as carefully, if not more so, than the scholar. Gregory Rabassa points this out in many of his writings and teachings, underscoring that close reading is also contingent on the faculty of "hearing" the text sing to you. The unfortunate person with a "tin ear" has no hope of becoming a good translator. It's the equivalent of a musician who can't read a musical score. For Rabassa, teaching literary translation was to model good reading and writing practices. The point of departure and arrival was always the text. He objected strenuously to the use of the term "target text," remarking dryly, "I am an old infantryman, and we dogfaces were taught to shoot at a target, and ideally to kill it" (2005, 4). Reading, some argue, is an act of translation. Reading highlights the subjectivity in the use of words, individually and as part of the context of a text and its component parts, the sentence, paragraph, or chapter. Each reader brings their own interpretation to the text and opens new possibilities. The translator takes this a step further by bringing the text into the framework of a new language, thus performing a type of alchemy.

Translation is built upon words. In reading, translators relate to words differently, looking at them through the lens of their semantic, etymological, and cultural functions. Rabassa describes this approach: "I have always maintained that a translation is essentially the closest reading one can possibly give a text. The translator cannot ignore 'lesser words,' but must consider every jot and tittle" (1989, 6). The word is the conduit to exploring meaning: the translator is called to follow the relationships between words, between words and their cultural context, between words and their evolution in history, and between words and their sounds. This process is one that Rainer Schulte and John Biguenet call "situational thinking," working out the possibilities of interaction and meaning in each text and coming up with a solution that approximates the emotional impact of the text: "In the translation process, thinking grows out of the situation within a text; it is not brought to the text from the outside" (1989, xii).

In his famous essay "No Two Snowflakes Are Alike: Translation as Metaphor," Rabassa defines words as metaphors for objects or other words. Furthermore, he writes, a word in translation is "at two removes from the object under description" (1989, 1). His favorite example, often repeated in class, is the word *dog*, which may elicit different images in the minds of the English, Spaniards, Brazilians, or Muslims. Our experiences with dogs will also inform our reaction to the word. Furthermore, dogs, like other animals, make different animal sounds in different languages, such as *woof woof* (English), *wau wau* (German), *hav hav* (Hebrew), *waouh waouh* (French), and *guau guau* (Spanish). Words not only describe objects or situations but also have spiritual and emotional connotations. Curses are a good example of the feelings behind words, and Rabassa points to the venom of different flavors that lurks behind the English "son of a bitch," the Portuguese "filho da mãe" (son of your mother), and the Spanish "hijo de puta" (son of a whore) (1989, 3).

Earl Fitz relates a story about the kinds of decisions about words that Rabassa had to make when translating the first sentence of *S. Cristóvão* by Eça de Queirós (1912; *Saint Christopher*, 2015), a project that Fitz took over at Rabassa's request after the latter accidentally fell down an escalator. One lexical decision, "once made, would resonate again and again throughout the text, becoming, finally, a basic motif" (Fitz 2018). This was the use of the word *serf* to describe a woodsman (since the Portuguese word *servo* softens the difference between *servant* and *serf*) in order to stress the political message of the novel. *Servo* appears over and over in *S. Cristóvão*, but also in different contexts, and Fitz felt that he could not use the word *serf* each time. Occasionally he substituted the word *servant*. He muses, "These latter cases had not yet appeared in the original text when Greg had to abandon the project. The decisions were left for me to make and based on my reading of Eça's text I did the best I could. I would ask myself this question: 'If Eça were writing his novel today, in modern American English, which word would he use?' Usually this would help me decide. Usually, but not always. Every translator knows this dilemma" (Fitz 2018). Fitz's process in taking over the translation was to study what Rabassa had done and to compare it word for word with the original Portuguese. He read the narrative several times until he "knew how it worked, how it developed, and where it went." He assimilated the characters, plots, and the important conclusion, which had to be done well to achieve the author's intended effect.

Rabassa concludes that the process of translation is one of choice. We must make a choice and put it in writing. Often the translator serves the text best when considering the choice that the author made. If there is a word in the receiving language that is an exact equivalent of the original word, then I try to use it. Often, there are multiple possibilities for word choices; when faced with words that are polysemic, or false cognates, one must tread carefully. Sometimes our innate preferences lead us to repeat words unnecessarily that later must be replaced. We should consider the role of articles, particularly if translating from Latin, Russian, or Chinese. Did the author want to say "the servant" or "a servant"? We are challenged to dig deep into our knowledge of the vocabularies of our languages to find the richest, most evocative words, rather than settle for what first comes to mind. Words change meaning and connotation over time, and choices made by earlier translators may not resonate in the present day. This is one of the strongest cases for retranslation, among others. The issue of choice leaves us open to the fact that there is always another one. In the end, we must accept that the perfect solution is a quixotic goal and finish the translation knowing that it will always be a work in progress in its journey across languages.

Translation Is Creative Writing

Like the creative writer, the translator starts with a blank page. And yet the literary translator's creative work, like the writer's, is embedded in her history of reading, the books that spoke to her, and the authors she translates. Translation, in Susan Bernofsky's words, "forces you to solve aesthetic problems that you wouldn't have to solve writing your own material" (Hond 2021–22). When a literary translation fails to engage the reader, it's because the translator is not a strong writer. A thorough knowledge of the literary traditions in which a work is written, and that work's relationship to other works, must figure into the translator's rendering. The key question is how the work should sound in English. Does the translation bring out the style, the genre characteristics, and the emotional ring that will convince a new audience? Mark Polizzotti, author of a 2018 manifesto on translation titled *Sympathy for the Traitor*, says of the debate between "faithful" and creative translation that "the other side believes that style is integral to the text, and that what you're trying to bring forward, knowing that languages work differently, is music. So, to make the translation give the same pleasure of the text—and I'm a big believer in the pleasure of the text—the translator will have to make choices and take some liberties" (18). Thus, we must ask, what elements of diction, syntax, tone, and figurative language must be considered? Does the translated book make clear the intertextual references and literary lineage of the original and of similar books in English? Those are questions that Rabassa posed to himself when translating Gabriel García Márquez's iconic novel, *One Hundred Years of Solitude*. García Márquez famously stated that the English version was better than his own original Spanish. He also thought Rabassa's method was to read the book through and then sit down and write it again in English. The way Rabassa describes in detail how he teased out the denotation of the words and the sounds in the novel shows that it was a much more complex process. García Márquez, according to Rabassa, "says . . . that it all came together in his mind, and he just sat down and strung together the words needed to express it. Maybe in some way I was simply translating in a way close to the way he wrote it" (2005, 97). Rabassa also layers in the importance of a translator's intuition. In addition to scholarship, careful text analysis, and wordsmithing, simple intuition guides the literary translator. What sounds and feels right for this text? Rabassa was always described as "intuitive." A good translator does not only have a flair for language. She is also intuitive, resourceful, and has a gut feeling for the essential qualities of the source text.

During the pandemic lockdown between 2020 and 2022, I was part of a working group of the PEN America Translation Committee charged with updating and rewriting the translation manifesto originally drafted in 1970 for the World of Translation Conference, billed as the first international conference on literary translation held in the United States. The call for action was an expression of the state of translation at that time and called for raising the status of the translator, expanding the role of translation studies in the United States, engaging publishers, and building translation resources. In 2020, the PEN America Translation Committee, in collaboration with City University of New York, sponsored the Fiftieth Anniversary Conference, which was titled Translating the Future. The conference, which was held entirely online, reflected on how literary translation had changed since 1970 and envisioned what it might become over the next half century. In conjunction with this, a small group of us volunteered to draft a new manifesto to renew and reset the calls for change—considering how the field had evolved—and to articulate what we wanted to see happen in the future. In the drafting process, many others were consulted and invited to contribute.

The 2020 manifesto, completed in 2023, consists of a series of calls for action, including a section on aesthetics and creativity. Here we stress the importance of moving beyond the old binary of original versus copy, stating that each translation is distinctive and constitutes a new text. We call for a recognition of literary translators as artists in addition to their role as curators and creators of new work. The central premise of this argument follows:

> Translators engage in the generative process of transforming one language into another. We are specialized writers who use formal, stylistic, and semantic strategies to create a text that corresponds, in terms of form, style, meaning, and more, to a prior text in another language. The translator cultivates a new voice for the text in the language of the translation by actively negotiating among diverse voices, literary forms,

and implicit hierarchies. The choices we make, including which texts to translate and the myriad linguistic decisions within the work itself, have ethical and political implications and are always in dialogue with existing literary and cultural traditions. Drawing on their immersion in the source text's language and culture, translators often create what might seem strange, new, or even transgressive in the translation in terms of theme, tone, language, and form through their play with syntax, dialect, register, loanwords, neologisms, and so on. The resulting creative disruption, rather than smoothing the text to make it palatable or accessible to readers, can impact the audience in ways that have historically contributed to the evolution of languages and cultures. (PEN America 2023, 12)

Kate Hedeen, a professor of Spanish and translation at Kenyon College who has been my partner in teaching several translation workshops, published her own "Manifesto?" in *Asymptote*, offering an alternative definition of translation, complete with footnotes.

translation is collusion[1]
translation is cahoots[2]
translation is concrete[3]
translation is commute your language[4]
translation is collaberration[5]

[1][translation translates to anomaly deviation divergence abnormality irregularity variation digression freak rogue rarity quirk oddity curiosity eccentricity transgression mistake disorder defect disease instability derangement vagary.]

[2][translation translates to suspect second fiddle copycat counterfeit ditto clone fake fraud false imitation make-believe sham imposter flimflam.]

[3][translation translates to hardened loss found set in stone solidified calcified deep-dyed card-carrying with copious translator notes.]

[4][that kind of talk translates to exchange switch swap transform convert go back and forth drive drive drive.]

[5][There is one privilege in particular that speaks to modernity's definition of the artist: inspiration. Although it dates back to the Muses and before, the modern idea of inspiration—that unexplainable gift bestowed on the artist—is often associated with the Romantics and lies at the heart of how creativity is defined. It is no coincidence that Romantic poetry and poetics also stressed originality and that imitation, once considered a beneficent and necessary corollary of creative genius, fell out of favor and was eclipsed by spontaneity and self-expression. (It is also no coincidence that all this comes about as the bourgeoisie solidifies its power and as capitalism becomes the dominant economic system in the West). Ultimately, inspiration legitimizes something as original, even though all creative work is always done in dialogue with other creative work.]

She concludes with this parenthetical observation:

> [It is not about being recognized by those in power, nor is it about making sure that we as translators receive the same privileges as other artists, nor is it about inverting hierarchies. Those in power, those privileges, and those hierarchies are the problem. Recognizing collaboration means rejecting the old dichotomies of original / copy and productive / reproductive that we are so used to hearing as translators. Thus, it allows us to expose the myth of originality and to begin dismantling the hierarchical relationships implicit therein. It allows us to consider all art as collaboration, and ultimately, as an act of solidarity. We must redefine not only what an artist is but also the creative act.] (Hedeen 2019)

The framers of the 1970 translation manifesto insisted, as we do now, that translators must be recognized and compensated fairly for their creative work. Their names must be on the covers and jackets of books. Rates of pay must reflect the labor that is involved. This is made clear in the calls for action for both the 1970 and the 2023 manifestoes. Rabassa recounts how, in earlier days, translation was "work for hire, like spreading manure on a suburban lawn, paid with a one-time fee" (2005, 94). He did not earn royalties for *One Hundred Years of Solitude*. While there has been progress in fifty years, we still have a long road to travel.

The Problems and Pleasures of Translating

Lydia Davis lists the problems and the pleasures of translating in her delightful essay "Twenty-One Pleasures of Translating (and a Silver Lining)" in her book *Essays Two*. I identify with many of the points she makes, the first being that the problems and the pleasures of the work are closely related: "the pleasure of writing . . . and the pleasure of solving a puzzle." The twist is that "in translation, you are writing, yes, but not only writing—you are also solving, or trying to solve, a set problem not of your own creation" (Davis 2021, 5). Many such problems have surfaced in my experience. One that comes to mind is the issue of very long sentences in Portuguese and Spanish and the reasons that lie behind that style of writing. In the case of translating the Venezuelan historian Germán Carrera Damas's long book on Rómulo Betancourt, the founder of Venezuela's short-lived democracy, the meandering sentences were a signal of Damas's erudition and a device to contain his many-layered historical and literary references. Nélida Pinõn's long sentences are a marker of her skill at achieving incisive shading and nuance in her description of characters and places. In the case of Carrera Damas, I toiled to condense his paragraphs into digestible sentences, using paraphrase in many instances. In the case of Nélida Piñon, I tried as much as possible to retain the length and flow of the syntax, to preserve the artistry of her style. No matter the solutions to these problems, compromise and a certain self-discipline are required of the translator. There are the occasional surprising and serendipitous (to again use Rabassa's favorite word) solutions, and many translators have found them. The other benefit of showing restraint and training oneself to compromise is one that Davis points out in her final "observations": the release of this restraint can find expression in our own creative endeavors. On the matter of sentences: first sentences are of utmost importance, and they are often the most puzzling to translate. First sentences set the tone of the story and can either hook the reader or lose her. The first sentence of Rabassa's translation of *One Hundred Years of Solitude* is often cited as a brilliant example of a first sentence that accomplishes what it is supposed to achieve: "Many years later, as he faced the firing squad, Colonel Aureliano Buendía was to remember the distant afternoon when his father took him to discover ice." The GRE subject test in English literature once quoted this line in a question asking the student to identify the text and the author (Shahmirzadi 2019). The implication was either that the English version has become part of the canon of English-language literature or that the test designers overlooked the fact that they were referring to Rabassa's translation and not to the original! Crafting good first sentences is a rule of good writing. The first sentence presents a puzzle to the translator that focuses attention on the aesthetics of a piece of literature as well as the underlying themes and tropes. The theme of time—and its inevitability and circularity—is a constant in García Márquez's work. This sentence points to the end of the main character's life and to his knowledge that this life is about to end.

Titles are always a puzzle. Earl Fitz and I translated Clarice Lispector's *Água viva* as *The Stream of Life* (not wanting to add an evangelical echo, as "Living Water" might have done), but on reflection it might have best been left in the original, the way it was done in the retranslation by Stefan Tobler. The title of António Lobo Antunes's novel *Não é meia noite quem quer* took me weeks to decipher, until I finally realized that the title came from the epigraph. It was Lobo Antunes's translation of a line of the poem "Entrapeçue" by René Char: "On a narrow path / I write my secret / Midnight is not in everyone's reach / The echo is my neighbor / The mist, my companion." The title of the first book I translated by Lobo Antunes, published by Random House as *South of Nowhere*, earned mention in Gregory Rabassa's memoir, *If This Be Treason: Translation and Its Dyscontents*. He says pointedly, "Here we are faced with editorial timidity because the title in Portuguese is *Os Cus de Judas* (The assholes of Judas). Staid Portugal, still imbued with forty years of the clerico-fascist Salazar regime, was able to shake it all off and display that blatant title on the cover of the novel in bookstore windows. . . . Since it's a military environment, it's a shame that the editors here weren't prepared to go all out and give the book a title based on an expression I remember from my own days in uniform (in Texas): The Asshole of the Earth. It would have fit in perfectly with the tone of the book" (2005, 142). "Middle-Ass of Nowhere" would also have expressed the idea of a place located in an obscenely obscure part of the world. However, the idea of betrayal was missing. I had suggested "The Judas Hole," and at one point the editors thought of "Where Judas Lies." I agree with Rabassa that the final choice was unfortunate. The title of Margaret Jull Costa's translation, published in 2012, was *The Land at the End of the World.*

Words themselves, as Lydia Davis remarks, always pose problems. She cites the examples of translators being called language nerds and geeks by Margaret Jull Costa and Eliot Weinberger (Davis 2021, 7). We enjoy searching for just the right word or phrase, one that will have the resonance and artfulness of the original. For English-language translators, it involves digging into the incredibly rich resources of the English language as well as investigating the literary lineage of the author we are reading. Rubem Fonseca was a deep reader of William Shakespeare in addition to modern American authors like Dashiell Hammett and John Barth. His use of vulgar language was woven in with the silk of Shakespearean phrasing (as in the title of one of his stories, "The Stuff of Dreams") and the bluntness of his American models. Re-creating that lexical weft required reading those authors to immerse myself in the texts that Fonseca drew from to create his individual and very contemporarily Brazilian style. Davis points out in pleasure 10 that "you become more and more knowledgeable about your own language and its resources as you work" (2021, 13). It hones our own writing and problem-solving skills that can be applied not only to our own work but also to translating.

Adhering to plot lines and developing character arcs can also be considered part of a puzzle, particularly in the case of detective fiction. The character named Shunsuke in J. P. Cuenca's *O único final feliz para uma história de amor é um acidente* (2010; *The Only Happy Ending for a Love Story Is an Accident*, trans. Elizabeth Lowe, 2013) wanders through a surreal futuristic Tokyo in a dreamlike state, which requires close attention to detail, topographical as well as psychological. The dystopian character of the tale, its excursions into dreams, and the ghastly accident that occurs at the beginning of the novel and is replayed with the smallest changes in four different places in the text demand attentiveness and the ability to fit together intricate narrative blocks. Staying true to the tone and register of dialogue and description also demands attention to narrative shifts. The same is true of translating Fonseca, Cuenca's role model in many senses. Fonseca created characters that appear in several works, including the detective named Mandrake, from the eponymous story ("Mandrake," trans. Clifford E. Landers, 2007) and the murder mystery

A grande arte (1983; *High Art*, trans. Ellen Watson). Maintaining consistency of character description and dialogue across the translated works is part of the translator's task, even if different translators are involved.

Translating is about relationships, which Lydia Davis lists as pleasure 4. Jorge Luis Borges's words come to mind: "A book is more than a verbal structure or series of verbal structures; it is the dialogue it establishes with its reader and the intonation it imposes upon his voice and the changing and durable images it leaves in his memory. A book is not an isolated being: it is a relationship, an axis of innumerable relationships" (1952; trans. Donald Yates and James Irby, 2007). If we work with living authors, and if we are fortunate, we can either talk with, correspond with, or now WhatsApp with them. If the author is no longer living, there are archives, letters, and papers we may consult. In any case, the author assumes a presence during the time we are in dialogue with their work, wrestling with it, rewriting it in another language and for another audience. Whether it is in real time or in our heads, there is a conversation with the author. In some instances, we might collaborate with a co-translator, as I did with Earl Fitz on Clarice Lispector's *Água viva.* During that project, we exchanged many calls and drafts, and we met in person a few times to work on the text. We discussed individual words, phrasing, punctuation, rhythm, and the tone of the elusive narrative voice. Lispector was no longer living at the time we did the work, so it wasn't possible to consult with her on the project, but we had my experience of knowing the writer and Earl's expertise on the lyrical novel to guide us. Most importantly, we were of the same mind on how to approach the task of translating Lispector, the guiding principles being love for her art and humility. In another case of fruitful collaboration, my "informant" for the translation of João de Melo's *Gente triste com lágrimas* (1988; *Happy People in Tears*, trans. Elizabeth Lowe, 2015) was Deolinda Adão, a native Azorean who worked with me on Azorean terms and lexical items for which no dictionary was helpful.

I resonate with pleasure 6, that in translating we are becoming a "shadow person . . . insubstantial" and speaking the author's words (Davis 2021, 10). The act of getting out of my own head, becoming the other for a while, is both energizing and restful. It also feels familiar to me, as a third-culture person, to blend chameleonlike into another person's imaginary world and into their culture (pleasure 7). It is a form of travel, leaving one's own world behind and living in another, perhaps internalizing something new that then becomes a part of us permanently. I revel in the lives and accomplishments of my literary heroines, primary among them Nélida Piñon and Clarice Lispector, and admire their courage, their daring, and their amazing skill with words. I can only hope that something of their creativity, curiosity, humor, and tenacity has rubbed off on me through the years.

The pleasure of doing research, what I call translation scholarship, is another reward of translation (pleasure 14). Many translators are not and do not wish to be academics or scholars—even if they do not hold overtly anti-academic sentiments—although, as Lydia Davis remarks, some scholarship is usually part of the job, and it can be pleasurable. Since I am an academic and a translation scholar who teaches translation, I coach my students that translation demands good research skills. I encourage them to write about their translation process, to cultivate the art of the critical essay on subjects related to translation, to learn how to review a translation, and to research their own translation projects with care. Most of the books I have translated have led me into subject-matter specialties that I would not have explored otherwise, such as Azorean immigration, the history of the Portuguese colonial wars, botany, geography, geology, Venezuelan politics, criminal law in Brazil, drought cycles in northeast Brazil, the Tokyo subway system, and bicycle repair, among other topics. Fact-checking is vitally important; we must be certain of dates, events, names, and other items of fact found in our source texts. If there are quotes, particularly from English-language sources (assuming that is the language we are writing into), it's incumbent upon us to track down the original, not back-translate, and make proper attribution. Maps and street directions must be correct unless deliberately meant to be misleading. I once had the experience of finding erroneous walking directions in Washington, DC, in the text of a Mexican writer I was translating, and the author was grateful for my catch. Terminology research is an essential skill, along with knowing the difference between a technical term and a common dictionary word. In the case of terminology, we must learn to use credible terminology glossaries, databases, and dictionaries. This circles back to the central building block of any translation: choosing the right word.

The Politics of Translation and the Agency of the Translator

Questions of power are endemic to the field of translation, and translators have a responsibility to exercise their agency both in the development of their careers and as actors on the global stage. Matters of nationality, language, and communication across languages are of critical importance in today's world. Translation plays a key role in everything from artistic expression to laws, scientific knowledge, global politics, racial and gender relations, and how peoples, languages, and cultures relate to one another. The translator's choices matter: which texts to translate, to translate in a way that makes texts available to new literary contexts and dynamic readings, and to play a role in counteracting deeply embedded historical social inequities. Quoting again from the call to action in the 2023 PEN America manifesto on literary translation, "We ought to approach our work in full awareness of the responsibility we bear given the history and geopolitical positioning of the U.S. and the global hegemony of English. We must resist flattening the gamut of human experiences by rendering them according to an inward-looking U.S.-Anglophone worldview. We call for the entire literary community to move forward with a critical approach that recognizes translation as the engaged, collaborative, and creative writing practice that it is." The call asks translators to "understand the cultural, social, racial, political, and linguistic contexts in which they work, and how translation can impact asymmetrical power relations. We challenge the tendency to assimilate texts from distinct cultural and historical contexts into a universalizing account of human experience" (2–3).

It is common knowledge that translators have been players and pawns in world affairs. Nazi Germany pushed translations of German classics out into the world to support their propaganda machine. The Salazar regime (1932–68) published translations from Portuguese into English for propaganda purposes and simultaneously carried out an intensive censorship campaign against Portuguese writers. The "Translation and Fascism" chapter in *The Routledge Handbook of Translation and Politics* (Rundle 2018) shows that there is a direct correlation between fascism and the manipulation of translation for political purposes. Translators throughout history have been persecuted, killed, reviled, and abandoned as well as honored for their work. The history of Bible translation is a bloody one. John Wycliffe (1330–1384) was branded a criminal for translating the Oxford Bible into English. Linguist William Tyndale was strangled and burned at the stake by Henry VIII in 1536 for what was considered a heretical translation of the Old Testament from Hebrew and Greek into English. Sir Thomas More had reviled him in rotund terms: "The devilish drunken soul [. . .] this drowsy drudge hath drunken so deep in the devil's dregs that if he wakes and repent himself the sooner he may hap, ere aught long, to fall into the mashing-vat, and turn himself into draf, as the hogs of hell shall feed upon" (Barnstone 2017). Today, translators are killed on the battlefield and left behind in war zones, as happened in Afghanistan. Salman Rushdie's Japanese translator was murdered, and his Norwegian and Italian translators were separately attacked but survived.

The importance of the work of translators is currently exemplified in the war in Ukraine. Russia's invasion of Ukraine in February 2022 triggered an urgent call by a Ukrainian translator, Kate Tsurkan, to get Ukrainian writers published quickly into English. The purpose was to push back against Vladimir Putin's false assertion, which became a slogan for his imperialistic designs, that Ukraine and Russia are "one people." Publicizing Ukraine's distinctive literary and linguistic heritage in English translation would be an effective act of resistance. According to a *New York Times* report of March 10, 2022, translators, writers, and publishers rushed in to help. Soon a group of dedicated people were speed-translating essays, poems, and war dispatches (Alter 2022).

Earl Fitz and I developed the concept of the agency of the translator in our co-authored book, *Translation and the Rise of Inter-American Literature* (2007). Our premise for the book is based on the key importance of relationships in literary and world affairs. Identities are formed from relationships between agents of cultural change and their translators. Writers, thinkers, and leaders in all spheres who influence and change worldviews do so in collaboration with translators. Translation played a pivotal role in the formation of a collective Latin American identity from the early days of the conquest. The story of the Mayan Indians Melchorejo and Julianillo, who were captured by the Spanish in 1517 and forced to translate for them, is one of passive resistance: small acts of mistranslation became their weapon against the captors.

Malinche, Cortés's translator and mistress, is held up as a national symbol of both betrayal and heroism.

The rise of new inter-American literature in translation was due to a series of events: the "Boom" of the 1960s and '70s; the Rockefeller Foundation's interest in sponsoring cultural exchange with Fidel Castro's Cuba during the Cold War; and the interest of the "big five" publishers, primarily Alfred Knopf, as well as agents, professional organizations, and literary journals like *Review: Literature and Arts of the Americas*, then housed by the Center for Inter-American Relations (now the Americas Society) in New York, in publishing new writers from Latin America. The translators who were the linchpins of this movement often acted as agents for their authors, with no guarantee of publication. Many of us were mentored and inspired by Gregory Rabassa, who insisted that we travel to meet and engage with new writers. Those of our generation working at the time, whose translations and essays were being published in *Review* as well as by commercial publishers, included Jo Anne Engelbert, Edith Grossman, Clifford Landers, Helen R. Lane, Suzanne Jill Levine, Alfred MacAdam, Margaret Sayers Peden, Barbara Shelby, Ilan Stavans, Eliot Weinberger, and Asa Zatz. Professional associations coalesced around translation. The American Literary Translators Association (ALTA), founded by Rainer Schulte of the University of Texas at Dallas, became an important voice for the work of literary translators. Literary agents also became gatekeepers and brokers for the new literature in translation. The late Carmen Balcells, the renowned Barcelona literary agent, and Thomas Colchie, a New York agent specializing in Brazilian fiction, pursued publishers and insisted on market-price contracts for authors and translators.

In our book, Fitz and I sought to approach the issue of translation through the idea of relationship in the context of the interaction between North, Central, and South American literatures. We argued that Canada and Brazil should be recognized as key players in the inter-American dialogue. They are often overlooked but are the source of some of the most sophisticated and innovative thinking on the nature of translation. We also focused on reception issues: how literature is read when it is in translation, for instance, and the effect that the translation has on the reader. As longtime advocates and teachers of inter-American literature, we examined the many choices that a translator makes at the textual level, where the word-to-word exchange between two different texts takes place, and the more conceptual problem of how very different cultures, literary histories, and critical expectations can be brought together for the purposes of mutual illumination. We were sensitive to the issues of what it means to know a foreign literature—in its original language and in translation—and of the role of the translator at the creative and interpretive level. In an age of almost instantaneous electronic communication and blurred identities, translation has become a fundamentally comparative problem. We believed that the historically troubled relations of the countries of the Americas, accentuated by issues of migration, language, and national identity, had to be faced in new ways if the Americas were to reach a more honest appreciation of one another's cultures.

Translation must also be understood as an agent of linguistic transformation. It has been the conduit through which new world cultures have related to each other and the ways they have assimilated European, African, and Asian influences and traditions. When cultures merge, words are imported and eventually find a home in the receiving language. As the creative agent who facilitates this exchange, the translator must be both careful and adventurous in using words for their transformative effects. Comparatists have long used the term *mirage* to refer to the impact that one culture makes upon another. Translation in this context takes on political dimensions that can transform reading audiences and the power relations between countries. Latin American citizens, for example, have known much more about the United States than Americans have known or cared about Latin America. Too often, stereotypes color this vision. Russell Baker, the *New York Times* columnist, made a comment that has remained a truism through the decades: "Americans will do almost anything for Latin America except take it seriously" (qtd. in Mead 1978, 2). This disregard has been one obstacle that translators have had to overcome: demystifying stereotypes. How one does this begins with choosing writers to translate who themselves work against cultural and political conventions—and then being daring in expressing their thoughts in words that captivate new readers.

The Role and Responsibilities of Readers

The section of *Translation and the Rise of Inter-American Literature* focusing on the role of the reader examines the influence of Stanley Fish and his reader-response theories and relates them to misreadings of Latin American literature during the Boom years. Borges contributed to playing to and with a new kind of reader who would engage with his games and fantastical narratives. Fish proposed that the reader is actively involved in the creation of meaning, which resonates even more strongly today as readers interact with digital texts. Fish's criticism pointed to fresh approaches to texts that create the terms of their own understanding, those he labeled as "self-consuming" and that could be identified in many of the "new novels" coming out of Spanish America (Lowe and Fitz 2007, 15). The questions we raised about Fish's theories had to do with the assumptions Fish made about the reader's knowledge of the cultural context of the source text as well as his assumptions about a culturally homogeneous readership. Most American readers did not have the linguistic, historical, political, or cultural experience that would allow them to understand new Latin American literature. Since the new receiving culture was unaware of the cultures of the source texts being introduced through translation, the interpretations of Boom writers were often skewed. This literature was inseparable from its social and political contexts. While a novel like Cortázar's *Rayuela* (1963; *Hopscotch*, trans. Gregory Rabassa, 1966) was transparently constructed for the reader's individual style of consumption, the underlying political layers of what was considered the light magical realism of *Cien años de soledad* (1967; *One Hundred Years of Solitude*, trans. Gregory Rabassa, 1970) would have been missed. Jorge Amado's popular books of the 1950s and 1960s featuring sexy mulatta heroines, such as *Gabriela, cravo e canela* (1958; *Gabriela, Clove and Cinnamon*, trans. James L. Taylor and William L. Grossman, 1962), were good examples of readerly focus on superficial issues, such as the seductiveness of the female characters. Works by politically and aesthetically challenging authors such as Pablo Neruda, Carlos Fuentes, César Vallejo, or Clarice Lispector were read first as examples of "exotic literature" that defied Anglo-American literary norms. However, in those Boom years, the work of translation pioneers (like Gregory Rabassa) who acted as agents for these largely misunderstood writers opened the door to later, more nuanced readings and inter-American dialogues that these texts and readers were initiating. In the case of Lispector, this has morphed in recent years into a kind of "milking" of her recent "discovery" by a new generation of critics, particularly Ben Moser, with his biography of Lispector and the translators he has appointed to retranslate her works. This present-day effort to create demand for her work looks too much like a marketing campaign for personal gain and reputation-building. The deliberate erasure of the work of earlier translations of Lispector by Moser and his publisher, New Directions, is a shameful dismissal of how new translations of an author build on previous ones.

The 2023 PEN America manifesto calls on readers to "actively seek to read works in translation and to read them as translation" (9). I would add that readers also have the responsibility to read translated works with an appreciation for their underlying social, political, and cultural contexts. The reader is invited not only to consume the foreign text for their reading pleasure but to learn from the text and to inquire further into its context. Only in this way can real dialogue begin.

The Yin of Translation: Feminist Perspectives

Gender issues in translation have shaped attitudes and critical viewpoints about the practice for centuries. A female translator must overcome old stereotypes, of course, but finding one's voice as a female translator can become an important part of the generative process. The enduring metaphors of translation have reflected the power relations and social hierarchies that place women in positions subservient to men. The use of the word *faithful* as a desirable quality in a translation subordinates the translator as the lover or mistress to the male "value" of the text/author. Judith Thurman (quoting Emily Wilson) writes that "the 'faithful translation' is a 'gendered metaphor.' It presupposes a wife-like helpmeet whose work is subordinate to that of 'a male-authored original'" (2023, 52). The language around "source" and "target" also has sexual connotations. The source text penetrates the receiving language and culture, with the translator in the role of stallion handler—or, conversely, midwife, who delivers the translation to the new audience. While translation has been a feminine praxis for centuries, male translators garner more contracts and attention. In academia, we are told not to do translations if we want to earn tenure, a situation that is changing, albeit slowly. Thomas Mann's translator Helen Lowe-Porter called it "a little art," although she became Mann's preferred translator and he wrote about her "skill and sensitivity" (Briggs 2017, 35). Married and the mother of three daughters, Lowe-Porter wanted to work and advertised that she was available to do translations from Italian, French, or German. She was sent a copy of Mann's German edition of *Buddenbrooks*, which started her career as his translator. She can be credited with cementing his reputation as, in the words of Todd Kontje in his preface to the *Cambridge Introduction to Thomas Mann*, "one of the few to transcend national and language boundaries to achieve major stature in the English-speaking world" (qtd. in Briggs 2017, 37). Even when Knopf was publishing his work after Mann immigrated to the United States in 1939, following the German occupation of Czechoslovakia, Lowe-Porter was scorned and considered unworthy, accused of making errors, being insensitive to nuance, failing to understand idioms, and omitting passages that were allegedly too difficult for her. It is known that she and Mann worked closely together and that Mann did have a working knowledge of English. While it is true that her translations are sometimes clumsy, even quaint, and too genteel for Mann's rough language, and that subsequent translations (including Susan Bernofsky's translation of Mann's *The Magic Mountain*) are by today's standards relevant and nuanced, in the context of her time, Lowe-Porter set a brave example for those who followed. Women translators (myself included) tend to approach the task of translation as if we were working at a craft like weaving, cabinet making, or sewing. Like Clarice Lispector, after I have done a lot of reading around the text, I translate without having read the whole book first. I find that this helps me focus my attention. My process is one of harvesting and sifting: I gather from my readings and research to inform my translation, and then as I revise, I sift and refine until the product feels right. Here is what Lispector says about her process in a *New Yorker* interview published in 2023: "I discovered a way to make it less annoying. What I do is I never read the book before I translate it. I go along sentence by sentence, because that way you're carried along by curiosity to know what happens next, and time passes. Whereas if you've already read it, it's a chore. It scares me when I see it that way, three hundred pages to go" (Moser 2023).

Susan Bernofsky likens her translation process to "varnishing a table, where you want to do a lot of thin layers, quick draft and not too much . . . [then] second draft, third draft, just multiple drafts." She couldn't do this with the thousand-page *Magic Mountain*, so it became a circular process of revision, revising while she is working. She describes "plucking out threads" of the narrative and following the words to create new solutions (Breen 2020). Swetlana Geier, the translator of Dostoevsky's "elephants" (as his novels were described), compares the translation process to weaving a tapestry and signals the importance of following individual threads to form the whole. Emily Wilson, the first woman translator of Homer's *Odyssey*, looked for ambiguities in the text and chose words that reflected emotional qualities, particularly of the hero, Odysseus. She labored over the word *polytropos*, which describes Odysseus in the opening of the poem, and finally came up with "complicated." She wanted to convey that there was something wrong with him: "I wanted the reader to be told: be on the lookout for a text that's not going to be interpretively straightforward" (Mason 2017). She sewed together "wavelike" W-words in the first half of the first stanza of the poem and "stormy" S-words in the second half of the stanza in a way that so impressed the *New York Times* reviewer, Wyatt Mason, that he wrote, "When I first read these lines early this summer in The Paris Review, which published an excerpt, I was floored. I'd never read an 'Odyssey' that sounded like this. It had such directness, the lines feeling not as if they were being fed into iambic pentameter because of some strategic decision but because the meter was a natural mode for its speaker." Of what she does with translation, Wilson stated, "I find there is a sort of religious practice that goes along with translation. I'm trying to serve something" (Mason 2017).

Translation can be central to feminist action: making decisions about what one translates and how to translate is essential to the work. Translation is a form of speaking truth to power as we move among politically situated communities. It is not the simple transfer of ideas from one language to another; often translators must face those who attempt to reinforce power relations and their own careers. Patricia Hill Collins, who has written on Black feminist thought and translation, states that progressive translators often use their social standing as power brokers to build subversive and transgressive spaces among people with shared interests and different languages. In an interview with Dennys Silva-Reis, she comments that

> my sense of an interpretive community makes power relations more central to the act of communication and translation. Power relations within an interpretive community regulate who gets to speak, who is listened to and what knowledge comes to represent that community to outsiders. Power relations shape who is silenced and who is heard. Racism and sexism work within particular linguistic communities, generating patterns of silencing and being heard that contribute to social relations of racism and sexism. Systems of power such as these turn apolitical linguistic communities into interpretive communities with differential degrees of power to speak on behalf of or represent a worldview. (Silva-Reis 2019, 223)

A feminist practice of translation is nonlinear, one of facilitating communication, sharing, and trust. This is a unique kind of ethical translation. Clarice Lispector turned to translation to supplement her income when she was a law student at the National Law Faculty of the former University of Brazil. She applied to the director of the Department of Press and Propaganda of the Getúlio Vargas administration to inquire about a job as a translator. There was no vacancy at the time, and she became a reporter and editor for the National Agency, where she translated documents and letters. From there, her path to becoming a translator and a writer was a winding one. From 1941 to 1977, she translated forty-six titles from English, French, and Spanish. The list of the authors she translated was eclectic: Edgar Allan Poe, Jules Verne, Jonathan Swift, Oscar Wilde, Agatha Christie, and others. She said about her translation work, "It's my livelihood. I respect the authors I translate, of course, but I try to connect myself more with the sense than with the words. These are mine, the ones I choose. I don't like being pushed, dragged to a corner, demanding things from me. That's why I felt a great relief when I was fired from a newspaper recently. Now I only write when I want to" (Book Center Brazil 2022). Some have noted a "certain symbiosis" between her translated texts and her own works that were published between 1974 and 1976, such as the similarities between Pascal Lainé's *La dentellière* (1974; *A rendeira*, trans. Clarice Lispector, 1975) and her novel *Hora da estrela*. Clarice Lispector was generous in allowing others to translate her works and believed that translating created community. While it was a way to earn a living, it was also a way to become a part of a larger world and to inform her writing practice. Literary translation and, ultimately, her writing were her pushback to the male-dominated hierarchy of the newspaper and publishing world, to the circumstances of her own life and the pain of her divorce, and to the patriarchy in general. Writing as liberation became a dominant theme in her work, expressed most explicitly in *Água viva*.

Translation and Readership in the Digital Age

The shift from paper to digital texts, the properties of those texts, and the ways in which readers interact with them raise new questions for translators and the practice of translation. The new space in which author, text, translator, and reader interact is virtual. A text may have an intended audience, but when the text is published and disseminated online, it is possible to reach a wider and less-well-defined audience than with print publications. Reactions to online literature are collected as data points that can influence the reception and dissemination of the work. The reader and translator are invited into more active roles as critics and coauthors—and sometimes take on the role of a character in the virtual domain. Translators can connect with their authors almost instantaneously through new communications media, enhancing opportunities for collaboration in the production and marketing of the translation. Editors and publishers also have greater mobility in the virtual space, and old networks have given way to less hierarchical methods of conducting the book business. I have found that close reading has been enhanced by using collocation software (or even search functions in Microsoft Word) that allows us to see patterns in words, syntax, punctuation, and style in the source text. Our inquiry shifts from "What does a text mean?" to "How does a text come to mean?" The digital analysis of a text, as a complement to traditional descriptive reading, examines the text from the inside out. The reading becomes one of making associations: seeking patterns and connections among words, images, and stylistic devices and their expression through semantics and sound. This process can reveal the aesthetic intentions of the author. In addition to opening new methods of reading, the discourse, themes, and techniques of digital texts invite translators to follow their authors' lead by drawing from the languages of film, visual media, and electronic communications in their writing.

Being able to do research online and having access to digital libraries can facilitate and speed up the necessary background work that the translator must do, bringing translation practice fully into the information age. The work focuses both on the texts and on the paratextual materials surrounding them.

The translator must track the digital world of the authors she works with, including their social media, online publications, websites, and now, more frequently, the literary works themselves that are generated for digital media. Online presence has been a leveling force in the translation world and has made international literature more accessible and more comfortable for publishers and readers alike. The public agency of the translator as curator is now more visible and politically impactful than ever before.

The Brazilian and Portuguese writers I have worked with in recent years are, for the most part, highly engaged users of social and communications media. We regularly communicate by voice through WhatsApp. Before she passed away in December 2022, I was in constant touch with Nélida Piñon, who generously gave of her time to talk about my work in progress on her novel *A casa da paixão* and who personally selected the stories that are to accompany the novel in the English translation to be published by Tagus Press. Rapid communications have made it possible to keep J. P. Cuenca, Noemi Jaffe, and Teolinda Gersão apprised of interactions with prospective publishers. When I was teaching at UMass Dartmouth in the spring of 2022, we used Zoom to bring many of the authors we studied into our classroom for discussions with the students in our Digital Brazil seminar. The students were encouraged to follow the social media presence of these authors and to communicate with them directly about their research projects. This immediacy of contact was a powerful tool in sharpening the students' awareness of the relevance of their work and the creative possibilities open to them as scholars and translators.

Teaching Translation

My first objective in teaching translation is to communicate the passion that I feel for the practice. I hope to light a fire in the bellies of my students. I speak to them of the translating life, its rewards and its challenges. I like to emphasize the qualities that a translator needs to work well: patience, perseverance, curiosity, a strong work ethic, and ultimately the ability to let go of each project and move on. There are specific skills that a translator must refine, such as the ability to read deeply, to listen carefully, and to choose words wisely. Above all, one must be able and willing to walk in the shoes of the other. Rabassa talked about the "*paredros* puzzle," borrowing the Greek term from Julio Cortázar, who used it to express the old Egyptian concept of otherness. At the same time, the translator "must turn the author into another possibility of her own existence" (Lowe and Fitz 2007, 158).

While the translator can be understood as the author's other, I have taught that it's possible to find a voice in translation. This is not exactly what Lawrence Venuti advocates as the "visible" translator. The visible translator, he argues, is one who employs "resistant strategies . . . to preserve the linguistic and cultural difference of the foreign text by producing translations which are strange and estranging, which mark the limits of dominant values in the target-language culture and hinder those values from enacting an imperialistic domestication of a cultural other" (1992, 13). Finding one's voice in translation is more than a political act. It is a function of how one interprets the original text and how one expresses the reading of it. This involves a series of strategic decisions that include word choices, finding the appropriate style to convey tone and register, and employing syntax so that it reconstructs the complexities of the author's creativity with their native language. The voice in translation is closely connected to the "ear"; one must hear the words on the page to re-create them in a new key. Finding a voice in translation also means writing the translation as if it were your own creative text. It will reflect what one's sense of what good literature should be like. In pouring one's own aesthetic sensibilities into the rendering of a translation, one's own voice will come through. The evidence of this is how translations of the same text will differ widely, and it is easy to spot which ring true and which fall flat. It is also supported by the distinct differences in how gender perspectives shape the approach to translation. Developing one's style as a translator is also partly a function of the choice of which text to translate. Which texts will help the translator grow as an artist? Does the voice of the original inspire and enrich one's own writing? I have found this kind of influence and motivation from the women writers I have translated, not least Clarice Lispector, Nélida Piñon, and (more recently) Noemi Jaffe. The translator must recognize when a source text is too flawed to merit their investment of time and talent. If the source text itself falls flat, the translator has the option to back away. Translators should not be in what Rabassa called the "silk purse business," making a silk purse out of a sow's ear (Wechsler 1998, 280).

Rabassa contended that the role of the teacher of translation boils down to being an editor, to examining the work of translators as well as each other's work in the classroom. He often said that "the proof that translation is an art is that it cannot be taught; you can teach a craft, but you cannot teach an art." I believe that a lot can be taught in the literary translation classroom. Aside from critical reading and creative writing practice, one can model values, cultivate an appreciation for the other, study the work of master translators, and lead students on a deep dive into the structure and subtleties of source and receiving languages. In commenting on the prose of H. G. Carrillo (who, it turned out, had fabricated his own life story, claiming to be a Cuban immigrant and a native speaker of Spanish), the Uruguayan writer Eduardo Galeano said, "Did you know that language can be read and heard and seen and touched? That you can smell it, taste it?" (Max 2023). These are the authentic qualities of language that we seek to find in translation.

Sutras for the Translator

I have practiced yoga for decades. When our daughter, Alicia, was three months old, Jon and I moved to Bogotá, Colombia, from New York City. We were staying at the Pension Halifax in the northern residential part of the city until we found housing and our household goods arrived. I spent hours walking Alicia in her pram down the tree-lined streets of that quiet neighborhood. One day I saw a little sign in a front yard that said "Yoga." I opened the gate and knocked on the door. A lovely woman answered the door in a sari, and the scent of incense floated out from her home. Doña Beatriz was the yoga teacher, and I became a regular student in her tranquil studio, with its atrium filled with plants and its aroma of eucalyptus. I have found that yoga, the practice of mind-body-spirit union, has helped me in both my daily life and in my work. It has taught me how to release bodily and mental tension and overcome the many challenges in adapting to life in Colombia with an infant. It has guided me through numerous transitions and difficulties since then. And yoga practice has also helped me cultivate a state of mindfulness that I feel is helpful in pursuing my teaching and translation practice. When I returned from Illinois to Florida in 2015, I took a training course and became certified as a yoga instructor. This experience illustrated how the principles of teaching and practicing yoga have broader applications beyond the yoga studio to the places I spend a lot of my time—the classroom and the writing desk.

Yoga is one of the systems of Indian thought known as *darsana*, derived from the Sanskrit root *drs*, which means "to see." *Darsana* thus translates as "sight," "view," "point of view," or "a certain way of seeing." The metaphor of sight extends to what is within: the texts written by yoga masters introduce ways of seeing that open ways of seeing inside oneself. The yoga sutras are a compilation of *darsanas* by the Indian philosopher Patanjali. Many meanings of the word *yoga* have come down through the centuries: one is "to come together" or "to unite." Another is "to tie the strands of the mind together." A further meaning is "to attain what was thought to be unattainable." Every step in the practice is a means to move to the next movement or point of change. Yoga encourages action with full attention, to create a state in which we are present in every moment and in every action. The student of yoga is taught to become aware of the holistic nature of being, realizing that we are a complex set of relationships between body, breath, mind, and more. In the sutras, Patanjali teaches that all aspects of human life, including relationships with others, our behavior, health, breathing, and our path of study, are important elements that we bring together to reach the next goal.

The sutras of Patanjali are divided into four chapters. The first, titled *samadhipada*, defines yoga and the challenges in reaching a state of yoga. The second, titled *sadhanapada*, outlines the process needed to change the mind from a state of distraction to one of attention—and the reasons for pursuing this state of mind. The third, *vibhutipada*, is about the capacity of the mind to achieve a state of focus. The last chapter of the sutras, *kaivalyapadah*, describes the potential of the highly attuned mind. The mind is most effective when in the role of servant. Thus, the idea of mastering the mind is reinforced. While this may seem an arcane departure from the practice of translation, I find that mastery of mind and body is a helpful tool for the work of translation. When I am immersed in a project, the ability to direct the mind toward it and sustain it without distraction is an effective strategy, just as breaks for exercise and fresh air are important for keeping the mind stimulated and the body relaxed. Searching the source text for its essential characteristics and underlying truths—and the ability to see what is expressed—is necessary to convey its message. Patanjali's sutra 1.7 states that "comprehension is based on direct observation of the object, inference, and reference to reliable authorities" (Desikachar 1995, 151). The translator is called to both study the source and do the necessary research to validate one's reading of the text. The practice of detachment (1.12) is helpful in separating one's emotions from the text while conveying the emotions expressed in the text to the reader (153). Sutra 1.14 encourages persistence: "It is only when the correct practice is followed for a long time, without interruptions, and with a quality of positive attitude and eagerness, that it can succeed" (153). Sutra 2 reminds us that "we are not masters of everything we do" (165). Humility, according to sutra 2.23, is an important quality that serves us well in our practice. We must recognize when we are not up to the task, or alternatively, that others may have found better solutions than ours. The distinction between what we see and the object that is seen is an important one. It is our reaction to what we see, or read, that determines the effects we create (172). That is why close reading and careful expression are so vital to the art of translation. And yet, as expressed in sutra 4.16, "the existence of an object cannot depend solely on any one person's observation. The river does not stop flowing because no one is looking at it." Multiple interpretations of a text are a reality that we can embrace. The body is as important as the mind in the practice of yoga. The sutras consistently instruct the practitioner to care for the body and one's surroundings, echoing the old Roman adage of "a healthy mind in a healthy body." Mastery of the mind, the body, and one's environment contribute to good practice in translation and in life.

Passing the Baton: The Possibilities of Translation

One afternoon, when I was visiting Gregory and Clementine Rabassa at their home on East Seventy-Second Street in Manhattan, Greg told me that he was no longer going to translate. The reason he gave was that he was having difficulty "finding the words." I still hold a visceral memory of the intensity of that moment. We talked about it for a while, and he reassured me that it was time to pass the baton to the next generation. He was quite serene about his decision. While I have not yet reached that point, when the time comes, I have his example to follow. The translation life is rich in possibilities, and if we as individual translators lose our capacity to find the words, our life's work will have contributed in meaningful ways to the transformation of the language we write in and to its literary canon. The impact of translation is to continue to revitalize national languages and literatures. Since translation is an interpretive performance, we can look forward to many new performances of texts that reach us from different languages and countries. Participation in this process is a celebration of the diversity of linguistic and cultural expressions. Artificial intelligence cannot replace the human translator. Our knowledge is embodied: we have trained for a lifetime to do the work, we have done the long apprenticeship with mentors, we have lived languages and cultures, and we have experienced them with all our senses. AI is disembodied knowledge. It has no context, no emotional or physical intelligence; it carries the biases of its programmers; it is a mirror of the minds that create it. It does not read as humans do. Instead, it sweeps the Internet for "content" (including translations, which are being used to train AI). As readers, we human translators are given the opportunity to experience the excitement we feel every time we open a new book. Reading is the pathway to living in multiple realities, to exploring the unknown, and to learning vital lessons that we can apply to our daily lives and our writing. Translation is also the pathway to self-discovery and affirmation of one's own complex identity. As travelers of the word and the world, we are in a constant state of personal exploration and renewal. We can look forward with anticipation to the transformation of the translation field as rising translators embrace their potential as humans, artists, and advocates for social justice. My hope is that the profession will continue to examine its aesthetic, ethical, and political practices in an ever-expanding global context by nourishing new writing and new readers in all regions of the world. The possibilities of translation will then unfold in ways that surpass our wildest imaginings.

Translating from the Portuguese

My future will not copy fair my past—
I wrote that once; and thinking at my side
My ministering life-angel justified
The word by his appealing look upcast
To the white throne of God, I turned at last,
And there, instead, saw thee, not unallied
To angels in thy soul! Then I, long tried
By natural ills, received the comfort fast,
While budding, at thy sight, my pilgrim's staff
Gave out green leaves with morning dews impearled.
I seek no copy now of life's first half:
Leave here the pages with long musing curled,
And write me new my future's epigraph,
New angel mine, unhoped for in the world!

Elizabeth Barrett Browning, Sonnet 42,
Sonnets from the Portuguese

Clarice Lispector: Everything Starts with One Word

I met Clarice Lispector (1920-1977) in 1974 on a trip to Rio de Janeiro to visit my parents, who were living in Copacabana at the time on their last overseas assignment before retirement to the United States. I had begun to correspond with Clarice in 1973, requesting her permission to translate stories from *Legião estrangeira* and *Água viva*. When I arrived in Rio in May 1974, I phoned her to make an appointment to visit her at her Leme apartment. This began a series of meetings on my trips to Brazil from 1974 through 1976, which led to a personal friendship and included gatherings at the home of Rubem and Thea Fonseca and Nélida Piñon. My favorite times with Clarice were at her apartment, where we would talk, drink coffee and freshly squeezed juice prepared by her cook, and play with Ulysses, her dachshund. She would occasionally interrupt our conversation, addressing me as "meu bem" and asking if I wanted sugar in my coffee. She laughed with childlike delight while telling me that her intuition informed her that I was pregnant before I had even walked in the door. She had asked the maid to put extra toilet paper in the bathroom because she thought I might have to pee frequently due to my condition. If the time advanced toward noon, she would declare that she was famished, exclaiming, "Quero comer uma galinha!" (I want to eat a chicken!), and we'd walk to the neighborhood restaurant for rotisserie chicken and a salad. Her appetite for simple food and for conversation was a delight to experience. In 1976 I did the interview with Clarice that was published in *Review* 24 (1979), along with my translation of "Sofia's Disasters" and excerpts from *The Foreign Legion*, translated by Giovanni Pontiero. A chronology by the late Professor Bella Jozef introduces the special focus on the author in *Review*. It chronicles Clarice's life from December 10, 1925, in the Ukraine to her death in Rio de Janeiro on December 11, 1977. In those days, before the Internet and instant news, I wrote Clarice a letter from Bogotá on December 12, 1977, in which I gave her a progress report on the translation of *Água viva* (the working title was then "White Water") and sending her my translation of the story "A procura de uma dignidade," which was to be published in an anthology. Of course, I never received a response.

In a 2023 article in the *New Yorker* titled "A Lost Interview with Clarice Lispector," Benjamin Moser claimed that the 1976 interview with Marina Colasanti and Affonso Romano de Sant'Anna that he had transcribed and translated is the "longest and most wide-ranging interview that Clarice ever gave, and offers a more rounded idea of her voice" than a shorter interview she did with Júlio Lerner (whom Moser describes as a fellow Clarice "obsessive," a telling bit of self-deprecation). I recently came across this article. Some of the questions and statements by Colasanti and Sant'Anna strike me as having a patronizing tone; they sound as though they are questioning a child. "Clarice, shall we start with a few biographical facts?" "Do you have brothers and sisters, Clarice?" "You've never said that, actually." "You don't remember that, Clarice?" "How many children do you have?" (Moser 2023). At one point, she asks for a cigarette after they ask about how she "constructed" *Near to the Wild Heart.* Then the interviewers suggest that she could make money by selling her papers to US universities, declaring that translations are a "detestable" way to make a living (Sant'Anna's word), although this is how Clarice supplemented her income. I am not sure that this interview reveals as much about Clarice as about the interviewers, who with their questions corralled her into places she had no interest in going and wanted to dodge. This is what happens when the ego of the interviewer takes priority over respect for the subject.

My interview with Clarice Lispector in *Review* was edited down from the full transcript. We talked about inspiration, her writing process, dreams, witchcraft (she had been called a "witch" or sorceress by some admirers), art as an antidote to madness, her dog Ulysses as a companion and character in her writings, nausea, city life, the status of women, and her life as a young girl. One of the topics that had to be edited for length, but which deserves revisiting, is what she said about the importance of words. Words are given the highest importance in Clarice's narratives. She described her process in this way: "Sometimes everything starts with just one word. A word will suddenly wake me up and then I'll write the sentence. I take notes upon notes, file them away, and then comes the terrible job of mounting them into some kind of meaningful structure. That's when I get terribly lazy. For me, the most interesting part is taking notes" (Lowe 1979, 36). Her process was a tireless reaching for the fourth dimension of language. Words, in her fiction, are symbols of reality to be compressed into images under the pressure of intense emotion. Words are centers of energy, and once found, they are repeated like a chant. Words also leave space for silence, the place beyond action that she sought to express. Finding that intensity, for words and silence, is one of the keys to translating Lispector.

Clarice's writing was often inspired by music, and she had a synesthetic imagination. She hummed the first bars of Brahms's Fourth Symphony to me when I asked her about the possible relationship between her writing and other art forms. "I always write with music playing," she replied. "I ruined my recording of Brahms' Fourth Symphony on *The Apple in the Dark*. I also paint, something not too many people know. But I don't show my paintings. I don't give them away, and I don't force people who have them to exhibit them" (Lowe 1979, 36). Clarice's living room walls were lined with paintings, many of which were portraits of her. She made a point of showing me one by Giorgio de Chirico, the renowned Italian painter and writer born in Greece (1888–1978). He did the portrait of Clarice when she was twenty-two. Her son Paulo Gurgel Valente gives the background of the painting in a chronicle in which he quotes a letter from Clarice to her sisters Elisa and Tania, dated from Rome, May 9, 1945:

My darlings,

[. . .] This afternoon was the last time I posed for De Chirico (pronounced De Quirico). He is famous all over the world. He has paintings in almost every museum: you've certainly seen reproductions of his paintings. Mine is small; it's great, a beauty, with expression and all. He charges very much, as is natural, but he charged less. And while he was painting a buyer appeared. He naturally didn't sell it. . . . But he came up with a story about making two paintings for me to choose. The next time I am in Rome, if my dear husband allows, I will then pose for him only, I mean, for the painting to be his (he would sell it then). My portrait is just of the head, neck, and a little bit of shoulders. Everything in miniature. I posed in that blue velvet dress from the Mayflower, remember Tania? When I take the picture of the painting, I'll send it. But you might not be able to see it well because of the colors that don't appear.

[. . .] I was posing for De Chirico when the newsboy shouted: The war is over! I also shouted, the painter stopped, one noted the strange lack of joy and continued.

After a little while I asked him if he liked having disciples. He said yes and that he intended to have some when the war was over . . . I said: but the war is over! In part, his phrase came from the habit of repeating it, and in part from the fact that he didn't even seem to be relieved, exactly. (Valente 2021)

Clarice was passionate about women's rights and knew the difficulty young writers had in breaking into the publishing world in Brazil. She was one of the first women journalists in Brazil. She had earned a law degree but, she explained, "I never practiced the profession because I'm not good at paperwork. Everyone thought I would be a good lawyer because I was always concerned with attacking injustice." She lamented the situation of young writers in Brazil who often had to pay publishers to break into print. The status of women she described as "leaving much to be desired; she is still enslaved" (Lowe 1979, 37).

In her writing, Lispector shied away from polarized positions on gender, presenting a fictional world in which her characters are expressions of a "libidinal economy," one that is energized by bisexual energy and freedom and that transcends the boundaries of what it is to be male or female, expressing a "pansexual being" (Lowe and Fitz 2007, 106). This is the opening cry of *Água viva:* "It's with such intense joy. It's such an hallelujah. 'Hallelujah,' I shout, a hallelujah that fuses with the darkest human howl of the pain of separation but is a shout of diabolical happiness. Because nobody holds me back anymore" (Lispector 1989, 3). Lispector's abstract and idiosyncratic prose presents many unusual problems for her translators. Her characters' musings about life and human identity always come back to language. Ronald W. Sousa writes of his 1988 translation of *A paixão segundo G. H.* (*The Passion According to G. H.*): "I have subordinated the rendition of many of what would traditionally be called literary devices to delineation . . . of the intellectual positions set forth in the book, and only thereafter have I endeavored to reproduce such features as style variation and artful use—or violation—of language norms" (Lowe and Fitz 2007, 104). G. H. muses, "Language is my human endeavor. I have fatefully to go seeking and fatefully I return with empty hands. But—I return with the unsayable. The unsayable can be given me only through the failure of my language. Only when the construct falters do I reach what it could not accomplish" (Lowe and Fitz 2007, 105). Giovanni Pontiero, another of Lispector's early translators, wrote substantive introductions and afterwords to his translations addressing her views on language, writing, and consciousness. His translations have since been criticized for a lack of accuracy in rendering the stylistic shadings of the originals, but he deserves credit for expanding the writer's audience when she was little known in the English-speaking world.

Água viva (1973; *The Stream of Life*, 1989), the book I translated with Earl Fitz, is the most condensed of her writings about female pleasure and writing. It was the inspiration for Hélène Cixous's theory of *l'écriture féminine*. Cixous wrote in the introduction to our translation that "pleasure is all *Água Viva* is talking about," and the problem the book presents is that "to say and to have pleasure is not simultaneous. To say something always betrays something" (Lispector 1989, xi). "What is tragic," Cixous states, "is that the word separates. There is a difference in language between the subject who has pleasure and the one who says it" (xi). Lispector's narrator wants to discover her own essence without the masculine associations with the word *possession*. Earl and I felt that this was the right book for our co-translation project, since we brought two gender perspectives to the writing as well as complementary readings and appreciation of her work. Having studied her work together in graduate school and explored it in depth in our own scholarship, we felt we could approach the task of translating this particularly challenging text with sensitivity for its nuance. We worked on drafts individually and then met occasionally to rewrite together, working at the word and phrase level. The critical response to our work was positive. In addition to Cixous's introduction, César Braga-Pinto wrote: "*The Stream of Life* is certainly the translation which is most akin to Lispector's 'thing,' since it does not try to translate it into a 'narrative.' . . . It thus echoes the original work without having to explain its meaning. . . . Unlike other translations of Lispector's books, the translation of *The Stream of Life* is not the result of the translators' attempt to fit Lispector's text into a particular interpretation. It is, rather, a re-creation of the author's original experience, its echoing, and at the same time, its celebration" (1993, 85).

I translated several of Clarice's stories. One of my favorites is from *A legião estrangeira* (1964; *The Foreign Legion*, trans. Giovanni Pontiero, 1986). My translation of the story, the first in English, is titled "Sofia's Disasters" and was published with the interview in *Review* 24. Here the protagonist is a schoolgirl who engages in a contest of wills with her elementary school teacher. It is the story of a first crush, a battle for the teacher's attention. The girl is both drawn and repulsed by the man, who "unchained" her "black dreams of love."

The more she defies him, the more he ignores her. The ultimate battle is waged through an assignment to write a story from a prompt that he gives, and the girl is determined to best him. She does more than tell the story; she finds its moral. Words are the most effective weapon in the end. Translating this story demanded close attention to the emotion of the piece in order to achieve the effects that Clarice brilliantly found to probe the feelings of a girl awakening to her power as a woman. The story also explores Clarice's theme of nausea, which, she told me in her interview, is physical nausea that she experienced as a child with lactose intolerance—not the nausea of Sartre, as some critics have thought.

Lispector's translators are invited to follow imagery in her narratives and to re-create the consistencies of that imagery. Her protagonists are driven by a quest for self-actualization, a new "order" of things that emerges from chaos, which is internal as well as external. The domestic chore of "tidying up" is a first step in finding that new place of self, as G. H. confesses: "I am afraid of this profound disorganization" (Lispector 1988, 9). G. H. persists in her search, as does the narrator of *Água viva*: "I want to write to you as an apprentice. I photograph each instant. I give texture to words as if I were painting, more than an object, its shadow" (Lispector 1989, 16). Clarice orders the quest with light and water imagery, mapping the conquest of new creative territory. Water imagery, of course, is central to the text and to the translation. There is a consistent progression of images from liquid to solid. The translator is invited to chart the changing course of the narrative and to follow its current. I recall that this is why the working title of the translation was "White Water." We changed it to *The Stream of Life* because implicit in the water symbolism is the dialectic of time–immortality: the creator must swim upstream against the relentless flow of time. Globes and towers are also prominent in Lispector's work. In *A cidade sitiada*, the city "was a manifestation. And in the clear threshold of dusk, the world was a globe" (1975, 52; my translation). In her books, there is an alternating sequence of towers being raised and felled, suggesting the halting way a work of fiction is written, in a rhythm close to that of the "narrative current" in *Água viva*.

Points exist in relation to other points in Clarice's books, forming image patterns that are central to her themes. Lucrecia, in *A cidade sitiada*, frequently visits the convent tower and hilltop to contemplate her "kingdom." The transformation of the maid's room in *A paixão segundo G. H.* is significant socially and existentially. Anticipating darkness and squalor, G. H. finds air, light, and space. This transforms her understanding of herself. These are but a few examples of how following the words, the themes, and the images in the work of Clarice Lispector informs the task of her translators.

Rubem Fonseca: The Morality of the Obscene

Rubem Fonseca (1925–2020) was a leading literary figure in Brazil from the 1960s until the time of his death. His gritty crime stories were metaphors of what he saw as the underlying decay of Brazilian society, and his cryptic short fiction, novels, and screenplays shocked and provoked readers with their graphically erotic content. Words took on a very different role in Fonseca's narratives. In 2003 he said, "I wrote 30 books, all of them filled with obscenities. We writers can't discriminate against words" (Astor 2020). A connoisseur of the curse word, Rubem used them with ruthless efficiency, often as equalizers between his lower- and upper-class protagonists who were thrown together in violent circumstances that erased social and economic differences. Although his writing was full of coarse language, Rubem was a deep reader who had a command of the Western canon and a wide-ranging vocabulary in both Portuguese and English. He could recite passages by heart from Shakespeare and from modern writers he admired, including John Barth and Donald Barthelme. He was an exacting mentor who demanded precision from himself and others, particularly when finding the right word or phrase. A former police officer, he used his life experience as his literary material, and he wrote convincingly of what he knew. His protagonists were detectives, criminal lawyers, and police inspectors, and his stories were often about crimes of passion or random violence, the kind he encountered on the streets of Rio de Janeiro. After he became a police officer in 1952, he was one of nine officers who were selected to spend a year studying business administration at New York University. This experience was formative for him, and he became immersed in the intellectual life of the city. He is perhaps the Brazilian writer who is most influenced by American literature and American movies, which he consumed voraciously during his New York days and throughout his adult life. On his return to Brazil, he worked for the private public utility company Light S.A., founded in Toronto by the Rio de Janeiro Tramway, Light and Power Company, where he became an executive until he retired to write full time.

I met him for the first time in his impressive office suite at Light in downtown Rio de Janeiro in 1973. As with Clarice Lispector, I had written in advance of my visit to request an interview and to discuss translating some of his stories. I was interested in his collections *Lucia McCartney* and *A coleira do cão* (The dog collar) and his novel *O caso Morel* (The Morel case). His work was beginning to raise the ire of the military dictatorship. In 1975, his book of short stories *Feliz ano novo* (Happy New Year) was banned and labeled a "literary obscenity" by the minister of education. A notoriously reclusive person who avoided photographers and the press, Rubem gave me access, and we developed a close relationship that lasted for several decades. His wife, Théa, and I became friends and eventually *comadres* (she and Rubem were godparents to Alicia), and she welcomed me into their home and included me in many family meals and social occasions. Rubem and I would spend long hours in his study in the Leblon apartment going over my translations, my dissertation in progress, and talking about literature and life. Occasionally we would go on long walks through the old center of the city, stopping for a *cafezinho* or a meal at his favorite restaurants, where he was treated deferentially by chefs and waitstaff. On our walks he would greet and be greeted by all manner of people from different walks of life, and he would regale me with stories about prostitutes, street crooks, and white-collar criminals, sometimes pointing them out on the street. He literally took me on walking tours of his fictional Rio and introduced me to his characters. He would address everyone, regardless of social status, with the honorific "senhor" or "senhora." He was adamant that the invisible poor and voiceless (the "Classe C" in his stories) be seen and heard. Before his death, he founded a library for Rio transit workers. In an unusual public appearance in 2013, celebrating his fiftieth year as a writer, he exclaimed to the assembled crowd, "Long live work!" "Long live reading!"

I enjoyed many visits with Rubem over the years, some in Brazil and some in New York, when he and Théa would visit. When I was in Brazil on the OAS dissertation fellowship, I interviewed him on November 25, 1976. We were sitting in a sidewalk restaurant in Leblon, near his apartment. The street sounds hummed in the background of the recording, and we were occasionally interrupted by the *garçon* asking us if we needed anything. Rubem drank *chopinho* and we snacked on the delicious cover items that are typically served in Brazilian restaurants: olives, *pão de queijo*, *mandioca frita*, and the like. Our conversation was wide-ranging, and he spiced his remarks with the expletives (most often "porra") that he used to punctuate his speech. I considered myself fortunate that he agreed to the interview, because he usually avoided them and hated being put on record. He warned me at the outset that he was full of inconsistencies and would probably contradict himself. Despite his joking and protestations, he gave thoughtful and detailed answers.

My first question was about his creative process. He stated,

> I am not concerned with creating a text. I start with an image in my head, triggered by something I see, a person, a gesture, a conversation, an incident. The story is there, ready. I must add words to it. What I really want to do is to communicate through images, which I do with writing screenplays. I would have preferred to work exclusively in film, but when I started writing I didn't have the means to do that. I work mostly through dialogue and give very little character description. I want the reader to participate as a co-author. What I write continues in the imagination of the reader. I don't labor over my writing. I edit almost nothing; I don't use dictionaries. My work is open, in the sense that Humberto Eco defined the concept.

He observed that reading requires more leisure and that a book is more subtle than a movie, although what attracted him about the language of cinema is its vast polysemy. Books are for the rich; the working person is too exhausted to read, and movies are a more accessible form of entertainment. I asked him to talk more about "the people" (*o povo*) he alludes to when talking about audiences and his stark contrasts between characters of the upper and lower social classes—what he called Classe A and Classe C. "I write about the people and thus for them. I try to destroy stereotypes and break down prejudices. I write about human hopes and desires. I would like people to be freer; I feel that the trend is for more and more control by those in power."

I asked about his aesthetic concerns, and he replied that "all art is driven by an aesthetic sentiment, otherwise it's just propaganda." He said that they conditioned him subconsciously: "I want to achieve the effect that the reader shares my social or moral preoccupations." Since violence is one of his major themes, I asked him how it came to take a central role in his stories. He replied, "I was always very aware of the violence around me. My family moved to Rio when I was seven. We lived in the center of the city, where we were assaulted by noises, lights, people being run over, muggings. Violence has always existed. As world population increases, violence escalates. Criminal violence is the result of commission as well as negligence and omission. With the rapid increase in mass communications, we are more acutely aware of the violence around us." *O caso Morel* is one of Fonseca's most violent works. I asked what led him to write it. He replied that his publisher wanted him to write a book that would become a bestseller. In this book he lays bare the crudest kinds of violence between people. "The sado-masochistic relationship of the main characters is how they stay connected," he said. "Here I worked on the problems of violence and injustice. It's the book I most dislike."

Love and death are two sides of the same coin in Fonseca's fiction. He believed that "death must always have a presence in a story. You are conscious of life because of the reality of death. Man is the only being that is aware of his own mortality." Love should have a greater role in life, but love is corrupted by power dynamics, the way people dominate and control each other. Women and men should free themselves from sexual politics. When I asked about the many prostitutes in his stories, he replied that prostitutes are omnipresent in the city: "They are the quintessential city character. They exist and should have a voice."

My work with Fonseca found its expression in the focus of my dissertation, "The City in Brazilian Literature" (1982), in which I explored the depiction of the Brazilian city as heaven or hell in the literature of the 1960s, tropes that have been present in the centuries-old canon of urban literature. In stories that form a broad mosaic of Brazilian society during the dictatorship, Fonseca creates a portrait of an urban society that is bent on destroying itself. I was particularly fascinated with the stories he was writing at the time, which were pieces of the Fonsecan social mosaic, and I published my translations of some of them in literary magazines, including *Fiction* (edited by Mark Mirsky), *InterMuse* (edited by Frederick Kaplan), *Translation*, *New World* (edited by Philip B. Johnson and Colin M. McLachlan), and *Review*. K. David Jackson's *Oxford Anthology of the Brazilian Short Story* republished my translation of "Intestino grosso" ("Large Intestine"). My dream was to publish my translation of *O caso Morel* (The Morel case), for which Fonseca and his agent, Carmen Balcells Agency, granted me the rights, though to this day the manuscript lingers in my drawer for lack of a publisher. (I haven't lost hope!) Later, Clifford E. Landers picked up the baton and translated many of Fonseca's books. My translations and interactions with Fonseca during our years of collaboration not only gave me greater insights into his work but helped me expand my range as a translator.

Rubem Fonseca wrote "Large Intestine" to explain his work. In this story, the character of the author, who refuses all requests for interviews, creates an alter ego who reveals his philosophy of life and literature to a naïve reporter. In the "interview," Fonseca elaborates on his uncompromising honesty of language, which has become a characteristic of most new Brazilian fiction. The Luso-Brazilian tradition had been characterized by a marked divide between literary and street language, a tradition that can be traced to the high and low registers of literary and vulgar Latin. In contemporary Brazilian letters, even those authors who avoid explicitly sexual or crude words in their narratives still use a speech-derived syntax that reflects modern reality. I learned to work with crude language by translating Fonseca, who weaponized it in the service of social and political criticism: "When the defenders of decency accuse something of being pornographic, it's because it describes or represents sexual or excretory functions, with or without the use of words commonly referred to as 'swear words.' The human being, someone has already said, is still affected by everything which reminds him unequivocally of his animal nature. . . . Metaphor is the result of it, so our grandparents would not have to say—fuck. They slept with, made love (sometimes in French), had relations, sexual intercourse, carnal conjunction, coitus, copulation, they did everything but fuck" (Jackson 2006, 463).

"Happy New Year" (1973) is one of Fonseca's most brutal stories in the collection by the same name that was censored by the dictatorship. What the censors did not comprehend in Fonseca's writing was his moralistic intent. In "Happy New Year," there is nothing that can prevent disaster. The characters are the grown-up orphans and street kids of Rio who are trained in social pathology and skilled at preying on the rich, who have ignored and brutalized them. The horror of the story lies in the first-person narrative voice that forces the reader to see from the protagonists' point of view and to experience guilt by association with the characters' wanton acts of social revenge, rape, and murder. The translator must pay close attention to this narrative focus and spare nothing in rendering the horror. "The Avenger," the title story of the volume *O cobrador* (1979), continues in this vein. Here, Fonseca adds ideology to the elements of rage and revenge present in "Feliz ano novo." The ideology is not given a label; the reader is left to define it. Fonseca suggests that no matter the ideology—and whatever is wreaked by urban guerrillas like the Avenger—the human condition will remain unchanged. Among the translator's challenges is to sustain the tone of irony and cynicism in the narration and to hold up the "mask" that Fonseca uses carefully to maintain an ironic distance. Authorial distance has thematic and strategic functions: by leaving his material unjudged, by posing questions rather than giving answers, by shocking and unsettling the reader, the author stresses the terrible uncertainty of life and the moral isolation of the individual. The irony that pervades Fonseca's stories belies his apparent objectivity but is easily missed by the careless or obtuse reader. It is because the rhetoric is so convincing that the government heavy-handedly sought to silence him. The translator is challenged to re-create that tone and to provoke the reader.

Rubem wrote to me on January 3, 1977, with the following news:

Não sei se você recebeu meu cartão contanto que o *Feliz Ano Novo* foi proibido pelo Ministro da Justiça, como "contrário à moral e aos bons costumes." O correio tem desaparecido com todas as cartas que escrevo e como a minha paranoia ainda não está muito forte acredito que é devido ao Natal e ao fim de ano e com o acumulo de serviço aos carteiros estão jogando as cartas no lixo, inclusive as minhas. . . . Meanwhile, a repercussão aqui tem sido imensa; não tenho todos os recortes, mas praticamente todos os jornais (grandes) do Rio e de São Paulo falaram no assunto, e também Veja, Manchete, revistas da imprensa nanica (Pasquim, Opinião, etc). Se houvesse repercussão nos States seria bom, não sei como consegui-la, você tem alguma ideia, alguma força para isso? . . . Isso porque estou pretendendo fazer uma ação contra o governo, não sei ainda qual, poderá ser a) mandado de segurança b) ação de perdas e danos e c) habeas corpus. O problema é que os advogados que consultei, alguns não querem patrocinar a ação por medo, cautela, etc. outros porque acham que eu perderei, pois a lei 1077, digo, decreto-lei 1077 liga a coisa toda à Lei de Segurança, um dos consideranda que diz mais ou menos assim "considerando que essas manifestações contrarias à moral e aos bons costumes fazem parte de um plano subversive que põe em risco a segurança nacional, etc." Essa dúvida, ou tibieza dos advogados está me botando puto e muito deprimido. Vão ser indecisos e cagões . . . Eu que tenho tudo a perder, não tenho medo de fazer a ação, qualquer que ela seja, e eles ficam valsando sobre as suas tecnicalidades, talvez metáforas jurídicas para o medo físico que sentem.

I don't know if you received my card telling you that *Feliz Ano Novo* was banned by the Ministry of Justice, because it is "contrary to morals and good customs." All the letters I have written are disappearing in the mail and since my paranoia is still not too strong I believe it's because of the Christmas and New Year holidays and with the accumulation of work the letter carriers are throwing letters into the trash, including mine. . . . Meanwhile, the repercussion here has been immense: I don't have all the clippings, but practically all the (big) newspapers of Rio and São Paulo have spoken about the matter, and also *Veja*, *Manchete*, the independent magazines (*Pasquim*, *Opinião*, etc.). If there were repercussions in the States it would be good, but I don't know how to make that happen, do you have an idea, or the strength for this. . . . I'm considering taking legal action against the government, I don't know whether it will be (a) writ of mandamus (b) loss and damage action (c) habeas corpus. The problem is that the lawyers I consulted, some don't want to represent me out of fear, caution, etc., others because they think I'll lose, since Law 1077, rather, the 1077 decree, links everything to the National Security Law, one of the clauses says more or less "considering that these manifestations are contrary to morals and good customs are part of a subversive plan that puts national security at risk, etc." This doubt, or weakness on the part of the lawyers is pissing me off and making me very depressed. They are all indecisive shitheads . . . I have everything to lose, I am not afraid of taking action, whatever it might be, and they dance around with their technicalities, which are perhaps legal metaphors for their physical fear.

I immediately wrote a letter to the editor of the *New York Times*, which was published on January 4, 1977, and pushed out my translations of his work as fast as I could to literary magazines. I felt that my efforts, however modest, were actions of resistance and support for Rubem and other writers being silenced. Fortunately, Rubem was not jailed, killed, or exiled, but clearly the effects of repression shaped his writing and activism for the rest of his life. His experience, and that of his contemporaries, has deeply marked the now two generations of writers who have followed him—most strikingly under the Jair Bolsonaro government, with its echoes of the dictatorship and efforts to curtail freedom of expression. The lessons of history don't grow old; they must finally be learned.

Nélida Piñon: Warrior Woman

Nélida Piñon (1937–2022) was one of the most generous people I had the fortune to meet on my journeys in translation and was the one who taught me the most about writing, persistence, and taking joy in the power of words. She was held in wide esteem in Brazil and was the first woman elected president of the Brazilian Academy of Letters. Her writing, while inaccessible to some because of its erudition and abstraction, was wildly provocative, and she confronted head-on issues of national politics, the rights of women, sexuality, and the complexities of family ties. In our interview in 1976, she had many things to say about writing, including that "working in literature requires nerves of steel." Writing, for her, was a personal liturgy. She sought to document the human condition and to chart the life journeys of a multitude of characters in different geographical settings of the Brazilian and Iberian worlds. She was a keen observer of people and situations yet always respectful of the privacy of others. Still, she did not hesitate to speak out forcefully for freedom of speech, freedom of expression, and human rights. Language was her obsession. She reveled in discovering words, and her erudite vocabulary was mined from her Galician and Portuguese heritage. She recounted that her mother once told her she should work on "speaking well" ("falar bem"). She asked what that meant, and her mother replied: "Speaking well is to show others what you are thinking" (Pereira 2023). From that moment on, she embarked on a quest for perfect expression: "The sentence has an ideal face, and I am searching for it. I am searching for something that I don't know but that is waiting for me." Nélida loved to talk (saying that she was dangerous because she talked so much), and her speech was a torrent of thought expressed in a melodic phonetic mix of Luso-Brazilian Portuguese with echoes of her Galician roots. She was a tireless researcher of words and their etymology, and her work charts the immigration of words across borders to create new language varieties.

I interviewed Nélida on October 19, 1976. The conversation began with her remarks on the miracle of the human voice. She thought of the voice as a "permanent miracle" that makes words possible. This speaks to the orality of her fiction, in which women's voices rise above and talk over those of men. She told me that she wrote as if her works would be performed on a stage.

This concept of writing as performance has stayed with me throughout my translating experience. She elaborated on the concept of the "temperature of language." Words for her were like three-dimensional physical objects, with shapes, textures, and temperatures. Every time she invented a new word, she created a new story. Her cultural and linguistic heritage was a point of pride. She described herself as "an American with an ancient past that enriches me." She had a past that "qualified" her to present "new visions of America." Crossing the Atlantic, she said, turned one into a different person. She wanted an America that was "free, open to question, and ready to make new languages." Her favorite American city was New York, which she viewed as the center of contemporary life. There, she said, she felt like a woman of the future. "I feel in New York as if I'm in the navel of the universe. What I will become will be revealed to me in that moment. It is my city of light. New York is a city with guts. It pulls truths out of me that I translate in my Brazilian way."

In my files is the typescript of a text that Nélida read at a "Debate on Brazilian Literature" at the Teatro Ruth Escobar in São Paulo in October 1976. The opening statement is her cry for Brazil to turn away from repression and authoritarianism.

Aqui venho, aqui estou, porque aspire à felicidade. Porque sou brasileira e temo o future. Porque me sei herdeira de um país dificil, sofrido, carnavalesco, que ignora a propria face, os lábios grossos, a sua história imersa dentro da história official, para dedicar-se a enaltecer o chamado homem cordial, resumo único de seu substrato pátrio. Aqui estou porque sou uma escritora que se recusa a viver circunstrita aos ingredients culturais selecionados por uma classe dominante. E finalmente, aqui estou, porque reconheço a importancia deste encontro, em que nos olhamos face a face, . . . desejosos todos de provar que somos uma raça ativa, não em extinção, como haviam anunciado, que pretendemos sim recuperar as palabras que estiveram perdidas, para conferir-lhes então novos registros. Aqui, neste teatro, nos caberão a estima, a confraternização, ainda que nos agridamos, ainda que apenas balbuciemos quando sonhávamos formular um longo coeso pensamento. Será este o preço que facilita e honra a vida. E isto apesar de nossas vísceras molhadas pelo medo e pela timidez.

I come here, and am present, because I aspire to happiness. Because I am Brazilian, and I fear the future. Because I know that I am inheriting a country that is difficult, that suffers, that is carnivalesque, and that doesn't recognize its own features, its thick lips, its history inside the official history, dedicating itself to raising up the so-called cordial man, the sole sum of its national substratum. I am here because I am a writer who refuses to live constrained by the cultural ingredients selected by a dominant class. And finally, I am here because I understand the importance of this meeting, where we can look at each other face to face . . . all of us wanting to prove that we are an active race, not in extinction, as they had announced, and that we do intend to recover words that were lost, to confer new registers on them. Here in this theater, we still have a reserve of esteem, of collegiality, even though we attack each other, even if we just stutter when we dreamed of formulating a long cohesive thought. That is the price of facilitating and honoring life. And this although our guts are wet with fear and timidity.

Nélida described herself as a "warrior" (*guerrilheira*), a high-class vagabond ("marginal de luxo"). Her texts, she said, are "irreverent, rebellious." As a child she loved to read adventure stories, listing authors such as Monteiro Lobato, Mark Twain, and Alexandre Dumas. These prepared her to tackle the metaphysical writers. She talked about her process of finishing one book and starting another. To do this, she needed time to purge herself of the finished text, "to erase a text created with great effort, to de-structure it." This for her was like losing her voice, becoming deaf and mute. "I have to take time to live a long time with silence before beginning a new text." Her characters, she said, gain their identities through language. They are "verbal situations." As such, they too disappear from her range of vision until she resumes her work to create new characters, new situations.

It was difficult to place translations of Nélida's work when we started to send out samples in 1976. I submitted a sample of *Fundador* to E. P. Dutton at the request of its president, John Macrae III, who wrote saying that they could not commit to the entire work since "Nélida Piñon's style seems to defy translation into English." I went on to translate several short stories, essays, and most recently her 1972 erotic novel, *A casa da paixão* (*The House of Passion*), with the support of an NEA literary translation grant. The novel had been translated by Giovanni Pontiero (though his translation was never published), and it is considered by many to be Nélida's best work. It is a pioneer in the genre of feminist fiction and has been praised by Toni Morrison, who heard of it when she was an editor at Random House. However, it is not well known and has long deserved a larger readership. Its lyrical treatment of a young woman's discovery of her sexuality, and her first sexual encounter on her own terms, is revisionist in terms of Brazilian sexual politics. Nélida describes the awakening of the female body in a unique and nonbinary way. The treatment of the young woman's voice is singular in that hers is the one that soars over the lines spoken by men who seek to dominate her. The idiosyncratic syntax and deliberate suppression of pronouns in the narrative (before pronouns were instrumentalized as a choice) make it difficult to follow who is speaking at first. It becomes clear whose voice is most important soon into the reading, and the voice becomes louder and clearer as the narrative progresses. Most of the lyrical description in the book is from the main character's perspective and provides insights into her psyche. It took many writings to render the dense, poetic language, with its unexpected lexical combinations, and to manage the subtle and frequent narrative shifts between characters and between dialogue and interior monologue. The prose is dense and has an unconventional logic. The novella and some of Nélida's more recent stories can be seen as parables of repression and silencing, and so the delineation of voices—and raising the voice of the female characters—becomes a paramount task.

My goals with translating Nélida Piñon's texts have been to expand the English with the richness and variety of her Portuguese and to allow the foreignness of the text to come alive while preserving its aesthetic integrity in English. Most of all, I wish to spark readers' imaginations with her voluptuous prose and the characters that she gave life to through the alchemy of her words. As one critic remarked after her death, she was Brazil's Scheherazade, a skilled and joyous teller of tales whose stories deserve to live many lives and travel over vast oceans. My last visit with her was in 2016. She invited me to dinner at her apartment in Lagoa. She entertained me royally with fine wines, a delicious dinner, sparkling conversation, and "festinhas" with her lapdogs. Her companion, Karla Silva, was there and showed me Nélida's archive, housed in a separate apartment in the building. I was invited to stay with Nélida on my next visit to Rio. We planned it for 2020, but it was postponed due to Covid. I spoke with her several times until her death, and her lightness and generosity of spirit are with me still.

Victor Giudice: Life Stranger than Fiction

Victor Giudice (1934–1997) is a little-known writer outside of Brazil and certainly one who deserves wider recognition. I met him in 1975, on my early travels as a graduate student, through the introductions of Gregory Rabassa and other writer friends. We became close and remained in contact for many years. I invited him to "The Week of the Brazilian Writer" in Bogotá, Colombia, in 1980, along with Bella Jozef and Earl Fitz. He published collections of short stories, among them *Necrológio* (1972) and *Os banheiros* (1979), and two novels. His works include numerous essays and short fiction in Brazilian and foreign publications. He has been translated into Spanish and some Slavic languages, in addition to my translations in English, which appeared in journals and in K. David Jackson's *Oxford Anthology of the Brazilian Short Story* (2006). I also wrote the preface to *Os banheiros*. His day job was at the Banco do Brasil, where he worked in public relations. He also taught literature at local universities. He had many interests, including playing musical instruments, graphic design, and photography. We spent hours together on my trips to Rio de Janeiro, and I often visited his home in Tijuca, where he would keep me spellbound, telling stories and playing the guitar. He had a very soothing presence and a habit of stroking my arm to make a point, which I found mesmerizing. His gentle touch was like that of a cat's paw. He was a large man with flowing white hair, a soft, high voice, and a thoughtful expression. His household consisted of his wife, Leda—a childhood sweetheart—and her sister, who I learned later was also his lover. His two children were grown and living out of the home. Later in life, he had a relationship with another woman, Eneida, who traveled with him to Europe to opera festivals. His personal story was retold in the story "Os balões" ("The Balloons" in *Os banheiros*), dedicated to me, in which a man convinces his bewildered and benumbed wife that his mistress should replace her in the marital bed and that she should move to the servant's quarters. The epigraph is a quote from the displaced wife: "If tragedy were as terrible as you imagine, I'd see it, the way I am, without glasses." Victor's wife did not live in the maid's room, but she gradually faded into the background, and after a while she rarely made an appearance when I visited. She allegedly had succumbed to mental illness, and I was told she spent most of her day in the bathtub. His wife and sister-in-law were always very hospitable; however, Eneida was very jealous of our friendship. She would come along when we went out to eat or meet for a conversation.

Victor told me in our interview that "fiction seems absurd because it's reality stripped of all its lies." He regarded institutions as absurd, and he sought to expose their absurdity in his writing. Most of his narratives are allegories of industrial man in no-exit predicaments. He inverted "normal" relationships, such as life and death. The fantastic, according to Giudice, is the "insinuation of the absurd into reality." The first story of his volume *Necrológio* (a play on *necrotério*/morgue and *relógio*/clock) starts on the book jacket. It is a Kafkaesque tale about a worker in a bank who gradually turns into a file cabinet. Some stories branch into the fantastic or science fiction, such as his supersonic romance "Salvataurus" or his utopian tale "The Points of Harmonisópolis." I compare him to Jorge Luis Borges as an exponent of the metaphysical fantastic. His erudition and elegant style, his mastery of plot, and his taste for the macabre align him with Edgar Allan Poe, Frederic Dannay and Manfred Bennington Lee (who wrote as Ellery Queen), and Agatha Christie. The atmosphere of eerie madness is made more powerful by the tight structure of the narratives. He stressed in our interview that music influenced him greatly and that he followed the structure of a sonata in constructing some of his short narratives. The ending has the same structure as the beginning, with very slight differences. His novels, he said, were structured like symphonies. He would listen to Beethoven, Bach, and Brahms while writing. He was also fascinated by the virtuosity of baroque artists and writers. This was something I had to pay close attention to. The premise of the story was presented to the reader again in another form. He focused on rhythm in his writing, saying that "the writer has to know when to change the rhythm of a narrative." Likewise, the translator must be attentive to these shifts in rhythm. Victor and I exchanged many letters over the years, and in one, dated July 23, 1983, he detailed his breakthrough in finishing a novel he was working on: "Suddenly, last February, I felt an uncontrollable need to finish the novel. There was a passage of about fifteen pages that intimidated me. One of the characters, a seventy-year-old woman, decides to recount the history of the city to the narrator. For this purpose, I invented a literary system to illustrate the woman's emotions: she starts to speak in prose and little by little, the language becomes rhymed until it transforms entirely into heroic decasyllables (the Lusiads). I wrote the fifteen pages during carnival. Sincerely, they are perfect."

Victor spoke of the fantastic as a genre that "gives color to fiction, in contrast to the black and white of reality." He wanted to make an impact on the reader. Science fiction, he said, was a modern form of romanticism. While romanticism escapes to the past, science fiction escapes to the future. While it is difficult to speak out against things in our world (he said this in the context of the military dictatorship), we can denounce the same types of things in the fictional world of the future. He felt that the languages of science and mathematics were the most effective in expressing the absurd, since those languages, which he described as "alienated," are themselves examples of the absurd.

Victor was preoccupied with his own feeling of alienation in the Brazilian literary scene in the years we had contact. In a letter dated April 30, 1978, he wrote,

> Atualmente estamos vivendo um momento estético singularíssimo, ao qual, compositores de música popular, diretores de cinema e escritores, sem falar na crítica, resolveram dar a denominação geral e única de brasilidade. Então, um filme de cinema, por pior que seja, é sempre considerado bom, se for dotado de brasilidade. O romance tem que ter brasilidade. O conto, idem. E, afinal, o que é brasilidade? Brasilidade consiste, de um modo geral, em vincular a arte que se pratica, direta ou indiretamente, a futebol, escolas de samba, marginalidade, classes sociais mais baixas, e principalmente, fazer girar a narrative em torno de acontecimentos circunstanciais. O texto deve ser completamente desprovido de quaisquer elements que demonstrem uma certa linhagem cultural do autor . . . Estou me sentindo mal com toda esta coisa de brasilidade. É uma ótica muito castradora. Sou filho de pai italiano e tive uma formação cultural meio européia. Cresci ouvindo música erudita. Nunca fui a um jogo de futebol . . . Sempre li autores europeus. Nunca fui ao nordeste, nunca frequentei os morros cariocas. Detesto desfiles de escolas de samba. Várias vezes já me disseram que sou elitista, coisa com que eu concordo. Que posso fazer? Abidicar de minha cultural devido a um modismo escorregadio que só se presta para ocultar uma série de deficiencias?
>
> We are in a most singular aesthetic moment, in which composers of popular music, film directors and writers, not to mention the critics, decided to come up with a single definition of "Brazilianness." So that a movie, however bad, is considered good if it represents "Brazilianness." A novel must have "Brazilianness," a short story the same. And after all, what is "Brazilianness"? It consists, in a general way, in linking art directly or indirectly to soccer, samba schools, those living at the margins, the lowest social classes, and mainly, turning a narrative around circumstantial events. The text must be completely stripped of any elements that show a certain cultural lineage of the author . . . I'm feeling uneasy with this business of

"Brazilianness." It is a castrating point of view. I am the son of an Italian father, and my cultural education was somewhat European. I grew up listening to erudite music. I have never attended a soccer game . . . I always read European writers. I've never been to the northeast. I've never been to the hills over Rio de Janeiro. I hate samba school parades. I've been called an elitist many times, and I agree. What can I do? Abdicate my culture for a slippery fad that is only good for hiding a series of deficiencies?

Our discussions around Victor's perspective on his work gave me insights into how to approach the translations. The problem of choice is the most difficult one for the writer, he would say. Everything—from the length of a sentence to punctuation to the words to describe a character or situation—is a matter of choice. Fiction, he maintained, was the art of constructing one story to tell another. Most of Victor's stories lead to death in a "necrology" of social corruption. Images of decomposition and putrefaction abound. Death, Victor said, was incomprehensible to him. It was a stupid waste and didn't make sense. He observed that people often die before their clinical death. Art, he affirmed, does not die. In 1996, he began to suffer the symptoms of what would later be diagnosed as a rare brain tumor. He did fulfill his dream of attending a Wagner festival in Bayreuth in the early stages of his illness, overcoming his intense fear of flying. By an odd coincidence, Terry and I ran into him, accompanied by Eneida, at Galeão Airport in Rio in 1996, when he was departing for Bayreuth and I was returning to Florida from a visit to Brazil. He died in 1997 at his home in Tijuca.

Machado de Assis: A Stylistic Exercise in Capricious Confrontation

The Library of Latin America series, undertaken in the early 2000s with Oxford University Press under the editorship of Jean Franco and Richard Graham, sought to make available in English translation major nineteenth-century writers whose work had been generally overlooked in the Anglophone world. I was invited to contribute one of the translations of the great Machado de Assis, whose identity as a Black man has been consistently erased by the Brazilian elite who embraced him as a national literary hero. The portraits that have circulated of him over the years have depicted him with almost white skin. He was born in Rio de Janeiro in 1839, the son of a mulatto Brazilian laborer and an Azorean woman. His paternal grandparents were freed slaves. He worked in low-level jobs, including in a print shop, as a proofreader, and as a translator. An autodidact, he began publishing his writing as a young man and soon gained a reputation in the literary world as a poet, critic, translator, and novelist. In 1896, he founded the Brazilian Academy of Letters, which he presided over until his death in 1908.

Three novels were selected by the series for translation or re-translation, including *Dom Casmurro* and *The Posthumous Memoirs of Bras Cubas*. The book I was assigned, *Esaú e Jacó* (1904; *Esau and Jacob*), had been previously translated by Helen Caldwell. *The Posthumous Memoirs of Brás Cubas*, a fictional postmortem first published in 1881, had been previously translated by William Grossman and E. Percy Ellis in the 1950s and Gregory Rabassa in 1997. Margaret Jull Costa translated the new Oxford edition with her mentee Robin Patterson. Another annotated translation by Flora Thomson-DeVeaux came out in a Penguin edition almost simultaneously with the Oxford translation. Both were reviewed in the *Los Angeles Review of Books* on September 22, 2020. The reviewer, Tal Goldfajn, commented in detail on these translations, favoring Thomas-DeVeaux's for her focus "not on reader comfort but a deep engagement with social reality" (Goldfajn 2020).

Indeed, Machado de Assis (1839-1908) was a brilliant observer of the contradictions of the Brazilian upper classes. At the end of the nineteenth century, they aspired to belong to the greater world and particularly to western

Europe, but they were members and beneficiaries of an essentially slave-owning society in a then remote—and in Machado de Assis's words, "a new and balmy"—country. Translating him requires working with a style that is both capricious in its ironic intent and confrontational in its attack on the decadence and folly of Brazil's upper classes and the stark reality of slavery. Machado transposes the plot of his *Esau and Jacob* from the biblical story of the conflict between two brothers. In Machado's version, the combative twins compete for the affections of Flora Batista. The historical moment is when Brazil is on the cusp of moving from a kingdom to a republic, and the twins are on opposite sides of the political divide: Paulo is the radical, and Pedro is the legitimist. While Flora's parents, and most of the country, are preoccupied with their political future, Flora is struggling over which brother to choose. This leads to her mental distress and death. As is typical in Machado's novels, there are observers to the events: Natividade, the mother of the twins, and Counselor Aires, a retired diplomat who provides a running commentary on events in his notebook. He masks his criticism with elaborately contrived compliments, a signature Machadian technique, while posing as an objective observer of human behavior. Dain Borges, in his foreword to my translation, remarked, "Like Aires, who has learned to disagree while appearing to agree, Machado knew how to move within Brazil's ruling circle while denouncing it in a style that its members found acid but agreeably philosophical" (Machado de Assis 2000, xiii).

It is always daunting to embark on a retranslation, especially when there are big shoes to fill. Helen Caldwell's translation was praised in the *New York Times* as deserving of "special praise for the ease, the witty grace, of her translation . . . an English stylist equal to the challenge of the original" (Fitts 1965). The reviewer cites one sentence that hangs absurdly on a pronoun: "Let him who is a mother cast the first stone." Indeed, this pronoun was used intentionally by the author and emphasized by the translator. The novel is described by Dain Borges as an allegory in which the characters are like chess pieces that elude Aires's ongoing analysis of their moves (Machado de Assis 2000, xii). The task was to keep an eye on the mercurial characters and the plot, which was an interpretation of real historical events at the time, and to follow the twists and turns of Machado's signature stiletto-sharp ironic asides. Dain Borges was an excellent guide to the historical context, with his depth of knowledge of this period in Brazil's history, and Carlos Felipe Moisés provided literary context for the project, which is summarized in his afterword. He comments on the intertextuality that is important to reading the novel: "The decision to imprint [the Biblical story of the twins of Canaan] on the title, is what forces us to compare the Carioca twins with the Biblical twins. In this subtle game are hidden successive and stratified layers of fiction upon fiction" (Machado de Assis 2000, 254).

My translation was described as "elegant" by Jenny McPhee in the *New York Times Book Review* (2000), and I hope to have done better than the "muddled effusiveness" that Jean Franco observed in her 1966 review of Helen Caldwell's translation. Flora Thomson-DeVeaux has been praised by numerous reviewers for her translation of *The Posthumous Memoirs of Brás Cubas*. Machado's narrator describes it as a book written with "the pen of mirth and the ink of melancholy." Like *Esau and Jacob*, which has 121 short chapters, *Brás Cubas* is divided into 160, a structure that our narrator says was devised because "long chapters are better suited for ponderous readers." Machado's narrator again aims his darts at the reader: "The book's greatest flaw is you, reader. . . . You love direct, robust narration and a smooth and regular style." Thomson-DeVeaux's lauded endnotes provide excellent context for the novel, and in them she occasionally questions her translation choices, which is a Machadian trait. It is the translator's dilemma to always question their choices after the work is in print. I can only hope that my writing captured to some degree Machado's ventriloquism and the brilliant artifices of his narrative deceits.

Wrestling with an Icon: Euclides da Cunha

The unexpected opportunity to retranslate another classic work of Brazilian literature was offered to me by Ilan Stavans, editor of the Penguin Classics series on Latin American literature. I have not translated many "dead" writers and prefer to work with living, contemporary authors. This offer was, however, hard to pass up, not only because of the book's importance but also because of the many difficulties it presented for retranslation. The task was daunting: *Os sertões* (1902) was considered to be the "Bible of Brazilian nationality," though it was also deemed by many to be an untranslatable book. Others thought that Samuel A. Putnam had done a masterful job of translating the book in 1944. In his translator's introduction, Putnam observes that "in making the acquaintance of Euclides da Cunha, the North American has an experience awaiting him which is comparable in quality to that of the European of the last century, listening for the first time to Walt Whitman's 'barbaric yawp'" (da Cunha 1944, viii). He hoped that his translation would contribute to the cause of hemispheric understanding and bring readers to an essential Brazilian work. Putnam was one of the first Brazilianists in the United States. His translation has been on the reading lists of Latin American history and comparative and world literature courses as well as those of Latin American and Luso-Brazilian literatures in translation. *Os sertões* was also translated into numerous other languages, including Spanish, French, German, Italian, Dutch, Danish, and Swedish. The decision by Penguin to offer a new version was based on the premise that the life of a translation is about thirty years; it was time to make the book available to a new generation of English-language readers. I found it curious that I, like Putnam, did most of the translation in the state of Illinois, which I playfully call the *sertão* of the United States, with its flat fields of corn and soy, extremes of climate, and notorious gangsters.

I viewed my task of retranslating an iconic text as one of rewriting it to make it relevant to a contemporary audience while preserving its "barbarous artistry and tropical exuberance" (da Cunha 1944, ix). Its power resides in how da Cunha elevated a local incident in a remote corner of the Brazilian backlands—which few readers would be able to find on a map—into an epic of great emotional resonance. The original English title, *Rebellion in the*

Backlands, was an embellishment by the first translator, and we felt it appropriate to revert to the original emphasis on "backlands" as the title's focus. Joachim Nabuco, the Brazilian abolitionist, described Euclides da Cunha's style as writing "com cipó"—with a liana stalk. The author claimed to wield the "crude pen of the *caboclo*, the Brazilian Indian" (da Cunha 1944, ix). The book has been classified as fiction because of how it arranges facts and incorporates imaginary elements. However, it is in fact inter-generic. Written by a polymath, it combines historical writing, scientific field notes, editorial journalism, the chronicle, the essay, facsimiles of military orders and documents, and political and philosophical discourse. The intent was to present a theory of Brazilian nationality in the discourses of art and science. The author felt that this interdisciplinarity was his major achievement: "a full synthesis of science and art, more than any single aspect, is the highest expression of human thought" (Santana 2005, 229). The book defies traditional classification and always provokes strong reader reaction, ranging from awe and fascination to irritation and horror. It is an account of the author's postcolonialist angst about Brazil's relationship with the "civilized" world—and that of the New Republic with the "barbaric" inhabitants of the backlands. Euclides da Cunha frames the Canudos campaign as a crime committed by the collusion of the Catholic Church with the Brazilian Republican government, the government of the state of Bahia, and the Brazilian army. The crime occurs in the context of the conflictive relationship of the Brazilian people with the physical landscape, both nurturing and punishing in its extremes. The division of the book into three sections ("The Land," "Man," and "The Battle") is inspired by Henry Thomas Buckle's environmental determinism in *History of Civilization in England*. The last third of the book is a treatise against war.

While the book's premise is shaped by Darwinist and positivist dialectics—opposing civilization and barbarism, the coast and the backlands, tradition and modernity, superior and inferior races—it is also surprisingly modern and relevant. The author believes that the role of nations is to create an educated and integrated society, that unrest is bred from inequality and lack of access, that the mix of races is the bedrock of the nation's strength, and that stewardship of the land is essential for human survival. The first section, titled "The Land," was my trial by fire. It is the setting and the protagonist for the Canudos story, and it inspired a whole genre of literature about the *sertão*, ranging from the works of historian and sociologist Gilberto Freyre to the novels and books about the Brazilian people by federal senator, novelist, and social activist Darcy Ribeiro and the postmodernist novel of the backlands by João Guimarães Rosa, *Grande sertão: Veredas* (1956; *The Devil to Pay in the Backlands*, trans. J. L. Taylor and Harriet de Onis, 1963). The section on the land challenges the translator with encyclopedic references to the work of social and natural scientists from around the world doing research in Brazil at the end of the nineteenth century as well as terminology and concepts from an impressive range of disciplines: geology, geography, botany, biology, ethology, anthropology, meteorology, and climatology. The character of Antonio Conselheiro is described with geological attributes as "an anticline that has been cast up by deep-lying layers of ethnic stratification" (da Cunha 1944, 117).

It is possible that Putnam envisioned readers with little knowledge of Brazil and its history. His translation contains extensive paratext. The lengthy introduction, the glossary of regional terms, and the detailed notes are evidence of the amount of research Putnam did to support the translation. His critical apparatus helped me immensely in producing my version. It was redundant to duplicate Putnam's documentation, so I attempted to make meaning clear in the text itself, limiting my notes to essential explanations of historical facts or regional terms. Ilan Stavans's introduction places the book in a broad comparative context.

My focus was on evoking da Cunha's idiosyncratic style. The adjective is the part of speech that drives his prose, which is at the same time baroque in its complexity and at times rough and blunt. The use of superlatives and antitheses is a distinctive feature, as are the Latinate vocabulary and the allusions to Greek and Roman mythology. Alfredo Bosi referred to "the torture inflicted on the intransitive verb" and other "infelicitous choices which call for a serious weeding-out" (Bosi 1973, 398–99). Interspersed with passages of intensive, reflective prose are sections of the unsentimental reporting of a war correspondent. Euclides da Cunha has been compared to Machado de Assis because of his way of addressing the reader in the first person, offering asides and opinions, often with biting sarcasm. The prose has been described as polyphonic and cinematographic, with multiple voices in dialogue, narrative shifts in point of view, and panoramic descriptions of the landscape alternating with closeups of the horrors of war. I used Alfredo Bosi's 1973 didactic edition of the book as the source text, which made few changes to the original other than modernizing spelling and punctuation. Bosi offers a detailed list of the features of his edition in the categories of phonetics, morphology, and syntax. Many have to do with the evolution of Brazilian Portuguese away from Lusophone Portuguese, such as verb conjugations and variations in word forms and spellings, which were not relevant to the English translation. What I did have to consider was the heavily Latinized vocabulary and the preservation of features of syntax and punctuation, particularly the ellipsis, which Putnam suppressed. Euclides da Cunha relied heavily on the comma, which he employed idiosyncratically, sometimes separating a verb from its subject with a comma ("But this train, did not exist"). The matter of syntax was a primary concern, as I sought to preserve the unique cadence of the source while seeking to achieve readability. The ellipsis is perhaps one of the most important stylistic features of the book as a way of drawing in the reader. It has been argued that Putnam's suppression of the ellipsis is his translation's greatest weakness, lessening its dramatic effect: "Because the ellipsis is so rare in scientific writing, when used it calls special attention to itself. It indicates that the author intends some sort of special emphasis on a particular passage, and it provides a space for the reader to enter the narrative and contemplate its implications. Putnam's translation, however, does not allow the reader this space" (Straile and Fitz 1995, 48). Other stylistic features that I sought to retain were set-off sentences, which in the original call attention to themselves and add emphasis, tone, and meaning. Putnam's translation converts this structure into more conventional English-language syntax. Putnam used many headers and sub-headers in his translation; I omitted them to guide the reader through the text without distracting from its integrity.

Euclides da Cunha used every rhetorical device he could find in his language to express the conviction that Canudos should never be forgotten. Putnam is most concerned with relaying content and information about Brazilian history and culture to his readers, while da Cunha sought to persuade them of the implications of the episode for Brazil's place in the world, its national identity, and the future of the country. In his introduction to my translation, Stavans described the book as "a meditation on journalism as eyewitness to history" (da Cunha 2010, viii). My goal was to bring the emotions of the experience of reading *Os sertões* to a new generation of readers and to provide a rereading that will contribute to a better understanding of Brazil and impart the author's vision of the world, which he sums up in the book's final line: "It is truly regrettable that in these times we do not have a Maudsley, who knew the difference between good sense and insanity, and prevents nations from committing acts of madness and crimes against humanity" (da Cunha 2010, 465). Not least, I also hope that my rendering has done something to enrich the English language through the process of bringing this unusual, lexically rich, and deeply layered work to a new audience.

João Almino: The Treachery of Memory

I first met João Almino (b. 1950, Mossoró, Rio Grande do Norte) when he was consul general of Brazil in Chicago. I was invited with colleagues from the University of Illinois, Urbana-Champaign and the University of Chicago to his beautiful home for a dinner party, where the conversation centered on Brazilian literature in translation. Later, he participated in a roundtable that I organized at UIUC titled Brazilian Writers and Their Translators. John O'Brien, who had founded Dalkey Archive Press, was a great fan of Almino's literature, and Dalkey had already published a few of his titles in English. Eventually O'Brien asked me to translate *Entre facas algodão* (2017; *The Last Twist of the Knife*, 2021), which was published shortly after John's death. Since those days, Almino and I have stayed in touch. During the Covid lockdown in 2020 we participated in a Zoom roundtable on my translation of his book for the Miami Literary Festival. Almino, a prolific novelist, has kept up his literary work while serving in various diplomatic posts around the world, including as Brazilian ambassador in Ecuador. Brazilian diplomats are known for also engaging in artistic pursuits. In addition to writing, Almino is an academic who has taught at several universities. He is the author of the five novels constituting *The Brasilia Quintet* and *Enigmas de primaveira* (2015; *Enigmas of Spring*, trans. Rhett McNeil, 2016). His latest novel is *Homem de papel* (Paper man, 2023). He was inducted into the Brazilian Academy of Letters in 2017.

My experience translating *Os sertões* served me well in working on Almino's novel. He was a great help, too, since his command of English is strong and we could discuss word choices in depth. Born in the northeast in Mossoró, Rio Grande do Norte, Almino wrote in this novel about the interior of his mother's home state, Ceará. He claims not to have written autobiography but to have invented biographies and memories. His personal experience, however, deeply informs his perspectives on the northeast and his treatment of language. In addition to the predictable issues of terminology specific to northeast Brazil, such as place-names, flora, and fauna, the regional sociolect and register had to be reflected in the English. Tone and register vary in this novel between the free indirect speech of the narrator, the words he records on the page (avowing that he is writing "quickly and without regard for style and vocabulary"), and the conversations he reproduces with family members, friends, and acquaintances from different time periods. The narrator began life as the son of a Black woman—a "subaltern," in his own words—who was a servant on a ranch owned by his godfather in the northeast of Brazil. Now a successful, recently divorced lawyer who lives in Brasilia, he returns to the land of his origins with the hope of rebuilding his life there. His real motive is to find out who murdered the man he thinks was his father. He discovers, in his obsessed search for the truth, that he may have been the love child of his rich godfather and therefore the half-brother of his childhood sweetheart, with whom he hopes to reunite on his return to the backlands. When the narrator recalls his past, he reproduces the speech patterns, grammatical features, and cadences of the language of the remote backlands. This spoken language has its roots in medieval Portuguese, with archaic verb forms and the use of the informal "tu" with third-person verb endings. The register reverts to modern, urban Portuguese in dialogues with characters from the narrator's present. The dialogues in this and other works by Almino are, in the words of one critic, "a dialogue with the emotions, which are, by their own nature, inaccessible to those attempting to recall them" (Monteiro 2010, 65). These emotions are brought up as much by the memories of people and events of the past as by the sounds and smells of the northeast backland; olfactory and auditory memories play a part in rendering emotion. The book brought back my own memories of the sounds, smells, sights, and tastes of the region, and they played a part in my rendering of the text, hopefully doing it justice.

The translation challenge, then, was to try to capture the cadence and rhythms of northeastern Brazilian speech as well as the register of underlying emotional tensions of old memories, which the protagonist acknowledges are treacherous. The voices in the novel are heard through the metanarrative of the protagonist, and the narrator is an unreliable witness. The use of several forms of the Portuguese past tense and constant shifting of perspectives create a montage effect that mirrors the instability of memory that the protagonist laments in his story. By deliberately writing an ambiguous narrative, João Almino (like his Portuguese counterpart António Lobo Antunes) casts doubt on the narrator's reliability by presenting his story as a kind of lie in which the storyteller seeks redemption.

J. P. Cuenca: Auto-fiction Antihero

I sometimes imagine J. P. Cuenca (b. Rio de Janeiro, 1978) as Shunsuke, the antihero of his novel *The Only Happy Ending for a Love Story Is an Accident.* Shunsuke is a Japanese salaryman who navigates a surreal version of Tokyo and falls in love with Iulana, a Polish hostess in a club in the Kabukicho district. The setting of small clubs, smoky pubs, and lantern-lit alleys is perfect for the mayhem that follows and culminates in abduction and death. In Kabukicho, visitors can go to kitschy sci-fi dinner shows or listen to rock bands play at Marz and Ashibe Hall. Daytime tourists can dress up in warrior armor at the Samurai Museum and learn sneaky feudal combat tactics at the Ninja Trick House, the interactive amusement center with ninja-themed activities like star throwing and swordplay. Written like a crime novel, the book's plot is full of odd events, and the story of voyeurism and perversion beckons the reader to follow Shunsuke and Iulana through the city to then witness the horrific accident that gets repeated, with the tiniest variations in detail, like a mantra throughout the text. Cuenca's interest in Tokyo stemmed from reading Tanizaki and Mishima and watching the films of Ozu or Kurosawa. The monster Gyodai is borrowed from a Japanese television series, *Dengeki Sentai Changeman*, that Cuenca watched on TV as a child. He later received a grant for a writing residency in Tokyo, where he began work on the novel. Cuenca told me that another influence on the plot of the novel was 9/11 and the horror of the destruction of the Twin Towers in New York City. Tokyo provided an apt setting for the futuristic dystopia that Cuenca wished to describe in his novel.

I met J. P. Cuenca when I was starting my work on the generation of Brazilian writers who were the children of the writers of the dictatorship with whom I had worked as a graduate student researching my dissertation. Cuenca, whose father is Argentinian, is a clear successor to Rubem Fonseca. We were introduced by Mark Carlyon, a British translator and scholar living in Rio de Janeiro at the time. I was gathering material for *Review* 83, "Cityscapes of Rio and Bahia," and I wanted to introduce some of these new writers to our readers. My encounter with J. P. has blossomed into a decades-long creative partnership that has given me unique insights into the post-1980s literary scene in Brazil. I observed that Cuenca was doing something new with the fictional representation of Brazilian reality. In his prose there are clear echoes of Fonseca's syntax, dialogue, and penchant for the taboo. The use of film syntax and techniques, like montage, movement of the camera "eye," and sparse dialogue, came from the Fonseca repertoire to find fresh expression in Cuenca. These were important stylistic elements in *I Found Out I Was Dead*, where I had to focus on short bursts of dialogue and exchanges of insults between the characters. Cuenca has become a master of auto-fiction, where through a series of metanarratives he places himself as the main character of his novels to give the illusion of veracity. This process began with *The Only Happy Ending for a Love Story Is an Accident*, where Shusuke's voice lightly disguises that of the author, and culminates in *I Found Out I Was Dead*—derived from his real experience with identity theft, when a man carrying his identification was found dead in an abandoned building in Rio de Janeiro.

The first of Cuenca's books that I translated was *The Only Happy Ending for a Love Story Is an Accident*, and this involved setting aside all the traditional ways of rendering Brazilian fiction to focus on the dystopian tone of the tale and its atmosphere of a psychiatric hospital. The characters are both surreal and mechanical, like robots that appear in sections of the book. The riffs on dreams and the graphic description of the accident that begins the novel demanded clinical attention to detail as well as a switch in registers to render the nonsensical verses declaimed by the mad Oikuda, Shusuke's father. I played with tonal variations and word combinations to try to achieve the very unusual effects the author created by writing a narrative in Brazilian Portuguese with Japanese inflections. In this novel, Cuenca makes his characters' words sound as if they were spoken by a ventriloquist; they are hollow, stilted, and weirdly funny. Translating them required an act of doubling the ventriloquy.

The doubling of character and voice continued in *I Found Out I Was Dead*, which was accompanied by a fake autobiographical film, titled "The Death of J.P. Cuenca." Both were released in 2016 and have been described as "parodies of auto-fiction" that dramatize the author's own persona. The book and film take place in "real" settings that blend reality with fiction and encourage skepticism about the character's authenticity. The author embeds himself into the plot and places autobiographical evidence, including letters, emails, press releases, personal documents, and the like, into the text. The fictional character is on a Kafkaesque journey to solve the crime of the theft of his identity while going on with his "life," suffering writer's block, and dealing with detectives and bureaucrats. The protagonist gives lectures and attends parties and films to promote his book, as Cuenca did in real life. He creates Facebook and Twitter (now X) accounts for his character, thus creating second lives for himself on social media and reinforcing the characterization of the book as an item of consumption. The author is clearly focused on how social media can affect the book's reception and on making public performance a dynamic part of the creative process. The translator's challenge is to re-create the illusions that auto-fiction achieves by simulating reality in a fictional frame. In a sense, I became another avatar of the author's and another ripple in the wake of the book.

Cuenca's novel *Nothing's Older than the Recent Past* is a "diary" of the Covid-19 pandemic written when he was in quarantine. It is yet another dystopian narrative that portrays a São Paulo in which the wealthy hide in their luxury apartments, fearing that the poor will try to invade their homes. They take refuge in Zoom calls and streaming video. The strangeness of living in lockdown, sleeping at odd hours, and having no personal interaction other than through digital interfaces creates the effect of a metafictional world that is both real and invented. The narrator is suspended between multiple dimensions: "Exile, whether in an apartment or in a distant city, reverses the meaning of things; life seems like fiction, the world we left behind, a dream. It's all memory, or almost" (Cuenca 2021, 18).

Cuenca was the target of right-wing evangelicals, who piled 143 lawsuits on him, and had his Twitter accounts shut down because of a perceived insult to then president Bolsonaro that Cuenca posted on his Twitter feed. This incident, from which he is still struggling to extricate himself with the help of international lawyers, attracted the attention of PEN America, which called out the Brazilian government and its enablers on tactics of suppression of civil rights that resembled those of the military dictatorship. Cuenca, like Fonseca before him, is a moralist, commentator, and satirist of Brazilian life. He is persistent and clear-eyed in his criticism of Brazilian society and government through his journalism, social media presence, and creative writing.

To do justice to translating him, one must follow him on all the platforms that he uses to raise his voice as a writer, citizen, and journalist. His perspective is one of a citizen of the world, one who is forever navigating world capitals and appearing at readings and conferences at universities and literary gatherings. This lifestyle has marked his writing with cultural and linguistic accents from Europe, Asia, and the United States. I have met and worked with him in New York, Rio, Vienna, Frankfurt, Dartmouth, and Gainesville. We communicate regularly through WhatsApp. This new way of relating to an author has helped me evolve as a scholar and translator and has kept me attuned to young writers' ways of thinking and being. Some of the great gifts of this work are the relationships we build with the writers we translate, seeing the world through their eyes.

Noemi Jaffe: Tales on Twitter

Noemi Jaffe (b. São Paulo, 1962) is a Jewish-Brazilian writer who produces much of her recent creative work for Twitter and Facebook. Her vignettes of daily life in São Paulo blossom like unfolding paper flowers on social media and provide glimpses into her domestic life, her strong feminist views, her love of country, her Jewish heritage, and her philosophy of living the good life simply and with open eyes. She often alludes to her Jewish heritage and once said something that particularly resonated with me: "To be Jewish is to give continuity to the narrative, and not just to be the child of a Jewish mother." I relate to that because of the strong connection to my Jewish ancestry on my father's side, to the importance of telling our stories and continuing the narrative. Noemi's narratives, in the various forms they take, compose a continuous story of her life, her mother's life as a Jewish Holocaust refugee in Brazil, and the lives of her children.

I met Noemi in São Paulo in 2018 through an introduction from J. P. Cuenca when I was starting my research on the children of dictatorship. She generously arranged a meeting of her fellow writers at a restaurant in Jardim Paulista. We were joined by Miguel del Castillo and Leandro Sarmatz. The lengthy, lively conversation opened my eyes to the concerns and themes that they were bringing into their work, their feelings of writing within and beyond a Brazilian and Western narrative tradition, and their fears and hopes for Brazil. Our personal connection was rekindled when Noemi came to UMass Dartmouth for our conference and spoke to what motivated her as a writer as well as the influences on her unique style. Noemi takes her role as writer and teacher seriously; she feels an urgency supporting her agency as a public figure, and her writing is a call to action on many levels.

Jaffe is a versatile writer, scholar, and literary critic working in a mix of genres, including novels, short stories, essays, and blogs that she began to publish on social media even before the Covid-19 pandemic. She is a director of the writing collaborative A Escrevedeira, a cultural organization that offers writing classes and events for the public and the literary community. She recently published a book on creative writing, *Escrita em Movimento* (2023; Writing in motion). Noemi has been compared to Clarice Lispector, and like

Lispector, whom she venerates as a model, she invites the reader to fill in the intentional blanks in her narratives. She experiments with the polysemous nature of words and with syntax and punctuation. In her story "O que vou fazer eu?" (2017; What am I to do?), she appropriates Clarice's story "Amor" to continue the narrative after Ana is distraught at the sight of the blind man chewing gum. This conflation of narratives is a precursor to her style of writing texts for digital media, in which the idea of the "original" is no longer relevant. The digital text lives in a "creative commons" and invites commentary and rewriting by readers.

In a Twitter post of January 17, 2017, Noemi commented that "tanto translation como tradução tem origem especial: trasladar e conduzir de uma parte a outra. é bonita a ideia de línguas como lugares" (translation and tradução have spatial origins: moving from one place to another and guiding to a place, the idea of languages as places is lovely [my translation]). She comments in an interview at the US Library of Congress that the origin of the word *text* is from "textile" and that writing is akin to weaving. I too employ this metaphor to describe my method of translating. Noemi's translators and readers are invited to work with her at the verbal loom. Words are what hold her narratives together, forming paragraphs that are always in lowercase, often with idiosyncratic punctuation. In *What Are the Blind Men Dreaming* (trans. Julia Sanches and Ellen Elias Bursać, 2016), a family story about her mother's surviving Auschwitz, she muses, "The future is certain when it doesn't exist, when words are the greatest thing we can count on" (106). Key words and verbal and syntactical patterns are breadcrumbs to follow when translating Noemi Jaffe. The stone in *What Are the Blind Men Dreaming* is, in the author's words, the "anchor" of the book. Both a real object and a metaphor, it gives a deliberate heaviness and rhythm to the prose, meant as a litany to recount her mother's torture in the camp when she was made to kneel with a heavy stone on her head for hours as punishment for stealing butter from the camp kitchen—an infraction she falsely confessed to in order to protect her cousins from certain death. The translator must assimilate the weight of Noemi's lived experience as a Jewish woman to give her narratives the right tone and register. Eric Becker describes her style as "deceptively unusual: it is captivatingly precise, with slow-building lyrical movements that are expertly grounded by a vaguely grim, often pained, tone" (2016). There are also lightness and mischief in her writings, giving them texture and depth, qualities the translator can embrace as joyfully as she does.

João de Melo: Translating Sadness

Translating João de Melo (b. 1949, Azores) is an exercise in finding multiple expressions for sadness, the theme that permeates his great novel of the Azorean diaspora, *Gente feliz com lágrimas* (1988; *Happy People in Tears*, trans. Elizabeth Lowe, 2015). Azorean by birth, he attended a school in Lisbon run by Dominican priests, like many boys his age did at the time. He served in Angola as a medic from 1970 to 1972, which served as the inspiration for his novel *Autópsia de um mar de ruínas* (Autopsy of a sea in ruins), and after the 1974 Carnation Revolution, he earned a degree in literature from the University of Lisbon. He has had a prolific literary career and become one of Portugal's best-known and translated authors. His 1983 novel, *O meu mundo não é deste reino* (*My World Is Not of This Kingdom*, 2003), was translated by Gregory Rabassa.

Happy People in Tears takes the reader on a voyage through five worlds —São Miguel, the island home of the family of nine that eventually emigrates to escape starvation, and the family members' respective destinations: Portugal, California, New England, and Canada. This long story of loss and an obsessive search for an elusive happiness is experienced and narrated through the voices of three siblings who have experienced the journey in different ways. It is a saga of family separation and alienation, the anxiety of displacement, and alterity in an increasingly complex and interdependent world. The book also offers a fascinating vision of Portugal during the Salazar dictatorship and the colonial wars in Africa, when the political collusion of church and state fomented a patriarchal society that is mirrored in the violence of the family ruled by an abusive father.

The Azores are geographically close to the United States and yet far off the radar of most Americans—this despite the relative proximity of the Azores to the US Northeast, the two-hundred-year-old Azorean communities in southeast New England, and the US military base located in Terceira, one of the islands of the archipelago. The Azores have remained remote and largely isolated. The Autonomous Region of the Azores comprises nine volcanic islands situated in the North Atlantic, 850 miles west of continental Portugal and about 1,196 miles southeast of Newfoundland. The beautiful landscape, shaped by wild storms, volcanic eruptions, and earthquakes, has reinforced the insularity of the place, which was gradually forgotten by Portugal after it was no longer a stop on the return from Africa, Brazil, or Asia during the centuries of Portugal's imperial expansion. The geographical features of the islands, and their separateness from the rest of the world, reinforce the trauma of the three main characters in *Happy People in Tears*, siblings who are prisoners of their poverty and domestic abuse at the hands of their controlling father. As two of the children leave for the mainland, Nuno Miguel, the main character, is placed in a seminary and Maria Amélia, his sister, in a convent. These are new forms of incarceration. The hold of the Catholic Church on the islands has been fierce, and the melding of secular and sacred—religious schools have been the only viable route to social and economic mobility for Azorean youth—deeply marked the language and its cultural referents. It takes a long time for the characters' voices to rise as they struggle to free themselves from their concentric prison walls. As they make their way into the world, the siblings face multiple hardships, and yet they survive, seeking meaning and resolution in their lives.

Adelaide Monteiro Batista, an Azorean scholar and the graduate school classmate with whom I studied and traveled in Portugal in 1973, specialized in the work of João de Melo. She notes that time and the physical features of the island are not just descriptive of the environment but metaphors of existential suffering and the conflict between wanting to preserve an island identity and becoming a part of the modern world. This epic dimension is central to Azorean literature and finds a culminating expression in de Melo's work. The push and pull factors of migration, and movement as a human condition, are important aspects that had to be captured in my attempts to translate the book.

I have not yet visited the Azores, which is at the top of my bucket list, but I did learn a lot about the archipelago, its language, and its culture from Adelaide during our graduate school years. She introduced me to her favorite Azorean authors, among them João de Melo, with whom she developed a close association. Later in life, Adelaide became minister of culture of the Azores. The language of the Azores is particular to the islands and their historical context. Because of geographical and cultural isolation, the language evolved separately. While not officially considered a different language, the difference in the dialect from mainland Portugal is in phonology, lexis, some grammatical forms, borrowings (there are many borrowings from English in Azorean speech), and formal and informal registers.

The unique nature of the Azorean dialect, the terminology particular to the islands, and the historical context of the Salazar period made this book particularly challenging to translate. The project required extensive research into the terms associated with the botany, ecology, economy, geography, geology, history, politics, culture, and cuisine of the archipelago. The main industries of the historical period were agriculture, dairy farming, livestock ranching, and fishing. Because the islands were settled in sporadic waves over two centuries, the linguistic and cultural aspects of the place are extremely varied. Capturing the unique environment of the islands, the clouds of the anticyclone that hang over the archipelago, and the character of the seven-thousand-foot-high Pico Mountain (referenced often in the narrative) invited me to transport myself virtually to the place, using all the digital tools at my disposal. I also found a wonderful Azorean informant, Deolinda Adão, director of Portuguese studies at the University of California Berkeley's Institute of European Studies and a specialist on Azorean culture and literature, to read my manuscript and validate my term choices and cultural references.

Aside from the linguistic and cultural considerations, de Melo's novel is polyphonic. The voices of the siblings are very different, reflecting their separate life journeys, level of education, and gender perspectives. Nuno Miguel is the "poet" and intellectual, Maria Amélia is a nurse, and Luís Miguel is a manual laborer. The last section of the novel is a duet between Nuno Miguel and his estranged wife, who brings the narrative into the present and alters the register once again. The polyphony comes not only from the narrative mix but also from the cadences of de Melo's lyrical style. Adelaide notes that the language of the novel is a fusion of "varied and opposing voices that develop and illuminate each other, renew each other, and silence each other in a process of mutuality and exclusion" (Monteiro Batista 1993, 48).

Finding a voice for sadness and for the ephemeral emotion of *saudade*, which becomes a place in which the soul resides in the Lusophone literary tradition, is the primary emphasis of the translation. The title, which I struggled with, refers to the immigrants who left the islands in tears. These were tears of loss and longing—but also of hope. The sense of the title also comes from an observation made by one of Nuno's aunts, referring to him: "What you have is a great wound in your eyes, son of my soul." The wounded eyes that shed tears are an expression of the Azorean soul. Once again, the task of translation was one of navigating sense, words, and style.

António Lobo Antunes: Translating the Voices in Their Heads

My first opportunity to translate António Lobo Antunes (b. 1942, Lisbon) came through Thomas Colchie, who in the early 1980s was actively engaged as a literary agent representing authors from the Spanish- and Portuguese-speaking world. He secured a contract with Random House for Lobo Antunes's *Os cus de Judas* (1979; *South of Nowhere*, 1983), and I was invited to translate the book. I was living in Bogotá then, and all the negotiations took place by mail (and occasionally a phone call). Erroll McDonald was an editor at Random House at the time, and I had the good fortune to work closely with him on the book. I learned a lot about the publishing world, about writing fiction, and about editing a book for a major trade publisher from him. We finished the editing work together during the summer of 1982, when I spent three months with Alicia in Woodstock, New York, at my parents' retirement home. Erroll took the bus from Manhattan and met me there, and we spent a few days going over the book line by line. It was an experience that has stayed with me my entire career. I also corresponded with Lobo Antunes from Bogotá, and he promptly answered my detailed questions (it took about three weeks for letters to cross between Colombia and Portugal) that mostly had to do with word choices, references to the Angolan war, and the free indirect speech narrative, which is his signature technique. The book was published in 1983 and was reviewed in the *New York Times Book Review*. My name was mentioned in the last paragraph, unusual for the time, and Alan Cheuse, the reviewer, described my translation as "lively." Given the rarity of any mention of the fact that a book was a translation in those days, much less any description of its quality, the recognition was thrilling.

In the review, Cheuse described the book in these terms: "Imagine a Vietnam novel in which the news from the front comes in the ranting recollections of a randy, self-hating, inebriated and almost psychotic veteran over the course of a long night while he attempts to seduce a young woman who is his drinking companion. If this sounds like mixing gin and Scotch, you've got it right. But it is precisely this mood of self-destructiveness and wrong-headedness that the novelist wants to recreate as he tells of the abandonment of an entire generation of Portuguese youth in the lost cause of colonialism and in the last gasps of fascism at home" (Cheuse 1983). It is this internal conflict that defines the narrator. It is audible in every line of the monologue and in the abrupt shifts of tone between rage and tenderness, the rapid alternation of the Lisbon present and the horrors of the Angolan war, and his memories of the slaughter and the beauty of the country and the people there. The book draws on the author's firsthand experience with the war. Like his narrator, he spent twenty-seven months there as a medic (he had a career as a psychiatrist after returning to Portugal). The main character falls in love with a female guerrilla fighter who is eventually captured, tortured, and killed. The war is the central theme of many of Lobo Antunes's novels, which describe the ravages of post-traumatic stress on his characters' lives and the lives of those around them. While the dominant mood of João de Melo's books is sadness, in Lobo Antunes the emotions that must be rendered are rage and despair. In *South of Nowhere*, the narrator's despair persists through postwar divorce and insanity to the night that we meet him in the bar with the young woman he is intent on seducing, when he feels "like a hermit who meets another hermit during a plague of locusts."

South of Nowhere was the book that first garnered international attention for Lobo Antunes, who is now acknowledged as one of Portugal's greatest living writers. My next opportunity to translate Lobo Antunes came from the late John O'Brien, who asked me to take on three more recent works. When he passed away, Dalkey Archive Press became an imprint of Deep Vellum, under the direction of publisher Will Evans in partnership with Chad Post. *Comissão das lágrimas* (2011), translated as *Commission of Tears* (2024), is the first of the three on the schedule. This book takes place during the civil war that followed Angola's independence in 1974. As a postcolonial state, Angola was left with economic and social tensions that erupted into a power struggle among the three predominant liberation movements. The Angolan factions also unleashed bloody revenge on the Portuguese colonists who had not been able to flee the country. An attempted 1977 coup against the Popular Movement for the Liberation of Angola (MPLA), which included former members of that faction, led to government retaliation and thousands of executions.

In *Commission of Tears*, Lobo Antunes revisits the history of Angola in the late 1970s through the chaotic dreams and memories of a damaged woman. The main character is Cristina, who is a patient in a Lisbon psychiatric clinic in the narrative present. Born in Africa and forced to flee with her family at the age of five, she has only vague memories of her life there. In a long, meandering narrative spun from the fragmented memories of Angola and the trauma she lived through with her family, Cristina recounts her early childhood. Her narrative is merged with the voice of her Black father, a former priest, member of the MPLA, and a torturer in the "Commission of Tears," the tribunal responsible for the executions of those who had allegedly participated in the failed coup against the MPLA. Cristina's white mother, a showgirl imported from Portugal to entertain Portuguese farmers in Angola, marries the ex-priest because she is pregnant with Cristina by the dance-hall manager, a man who exploited and raped her. The story weaves together the three voices of daughter, father, and mother as they remember the terrors of Angola. Their brokenness mirrors that of the country that was being destroyed around them.

Cristina, who is plagued by voices that tell her to do bad things, gives us several clues to reading this novel. She says in the seventh chapter that her job is to "translate" the voices in her head, the cajoling and taunting voices that come from leaves and objects around her and that question her relentlessly. She calls these voices "guides" that prompt her to "write" the book, and she characterizes her narrative as a coiled spring that slowly unravels. The interwoven stories, which wander along crooked paths, are no more reliable than the voices that "dictate" them to Cristina. The voices dissociate her from her lived traumas and free her to question and face them from different points of view. Cristina refuses to speak to her doctors or parents and writes that she has difficulty reading and writing. What we read as a written narrative, and what Cristina describes as her book, is played out entirely in her head. The setting is equally ambiguous: the action toggles back and forth between Lisbon and Luanda and remote locations in Portugal and Angola. The depiction of space is filtered through memory and is likened to waves in the Moçâmedes Sea and to the ever-rustling palm leaves that echo in Cristina's memory.

The treatment of time in Lobo Antunes's novels, one of his central themes, is where I focused much of my attention. Time and place are in constant movement, and there is no clear plot structure, temporal logic, or even direct connections between the characters. Punctuation is unconventional and inconsistent. The action unfolds in an eternal present, which highlights the characters' suffering. The effect of this cinematic montage technique also allows for parallel views of the internal and external worlds of the characters. Jeff Love, translator of Lobo Antunes's *Até que as pedras se tornem mais leves que a água* (2017; *Until Stones Become Lighter than Water*, 2019), notes that he "radically attenuates the complicated verbal system of Portuguese by favoring infinitival structures over finite tensed ones" (Lobo Antunes 2019, xvi). The use of the personal infinitive creates a "presencing effect," giving the illusion of spoken performance that occurs with the act of reading. Like Love, I used the English gerund form to achieve this, and the effect in both English and Portuguese is unusual. Other forms of the past tense in the original Portuguese text, including the preterite, imperfect, pluperfect, and imperfect subjunctive, add to the effect of blurring time sequences in the novel. The gerund as a translation of the Portuguese personal infinitive achieves the effect of action that is unaffected by time. Love also comments on the suppression of the verb "to be" in Lobo Antunes's style, which also disrupts the temporal order. He describes it as a "prose of a somewhat hidden simultaneity" (xvii). It was important to retain this aspect of verbal incongruence in my translation, as odd as it seems in both Portuguese and English. Fortunately, the editors I worked with on the Lobo Antunes books did not attempt to smooth this out.

Race and racial tensions are a constant in the Angolan novels. Lobo Antunes uses designations for race that mirror the structural racism of colonized countries. The term *mestiço*, usually associated with Brazil, is in the Angolan context someone of mixed blood, including African, Caucasian, and Indigenous descent. I used the term *mestizo*. The word *cafuzo* translates as "Black Indian," a term used in the Spanish and Portuguese empires for a person of mixed Indigenous and African ancestry. *Mulatto/a* is a person of mixed African and Caucasian blood, and today the term is considered dated and sometimes pejorative.

I found that the best way to translate Lobo Antunes, particularly the later novels (including *Commission of Tears*), was to follow the voices in his characters' heads as they spilled out their stories in his signature time-blurring style. This process of unraveling the narrative skein, the taking apart of a tightly held story, was in the end what made everything clear. Sadly, Lobo

Antunes was not available for consultation on this book owing to ill health. He sent a message through his publisher in Lisbon that he trusted my judgment. I am grateful for that trust.

Teolinda Gersão

My relationship with Teolinda (b. Coimbra, 1940) began through an opportunity to publish my translation of one of her short stories in the 2019 edition of Dalkey Archive Press's series titled Best European Fiction. Working with Teolinda is a pleasure: she is communicative, responsive, full of life, and very present on the literary scene in Europe and Brazil. She maintains an active voice on social media and keeps up a flow of information on her own and other literary events in Portugal and elsewhere. In contrast to the male-dominated world of António Lobo Antunes, in which anger and remorse are the primary emotional tones, Teolinda's narrative world is that of women who find their voice in public, in relationships, and as writers. The erasure of women, and their ways of claiming their voice through acts of resistance, is the grand theme of her fiction. The violence in her novels is perpetrated by women through silence, sensuality, retreat into dream worlds, ending pregnancies, or—like Julia in *O retorno de Júlia Mann a Paraty* (2021; The return of Júlia Mann to Paraty)—playing Brazilian music on the piano in her austere German home. Teolinda's first novel, *O silêncio* (1981; *Silence*), which won the Pen Club award that year, thematizes the political silence and censorship of the Salazar regime as well as the yoke of the patriarchy. She forges a new language for women in her writing that finds expression for women's complex inner worlds and their attempts to break out of the prison house of the language of male hegemony. Two of her novels have been translated into English. Margaret Jull Costa translated *A árvore das palavras* (2010; *The Word Tree*), which won the 2012 Calouste Gulbenkian Prize, and *A cidade de Ulisses* (2011), published by Dalkey Archive Press in 2017 as *City of Ulysses*, was translated by Jethro Soutar and Annie McDermott. Teolinda produced primarily short fiction from 2000 to 2010 and acknowledged in an interview that the short story form was for her a destination rather than a point of departure. Margaret Jull Costa translated many of her stories, which appeared in literary journals in print and online, including in *Words Without Borders* and with Two Lines Press.

My experience translating her story "Detrás dis Sonhos" ("Behind the Dreams") was an exercise in finding a tone for the female protagonist's quiet desperation. As in the novel *Silence*, the story is told by the woman's husband. In *Silence*, Paulo is the narrator, but the focus is on his ex-lover Cecilia's struggle to assert herself in their relationship, which she eventually leaves. In "Behind the Dreams," the husband's dismissive and dry account of his wife's mental decline, and his eventual abandonment of the marriage, is an act of removing her from his life and disavowing his guilt in the matter. The wife's voice comes out as she tells her dreams to her disinterested spouse. Finding the shift of tone and register to distinguish the male narrative from the female voice (that is heard in only one paragraph, in quotation marks, as reported by the husband) was the main task I faced. The husband is disingenuous and self-pitying in his reporting as he seeks to make a case for leaving his suffering wife.

The next project with Teolinda is the translation of *O retorno de Júlia Mann a Paraty*. This novel appeals to me because of its setting in Germany in the first half of the twentieth century (Teolinda studied in Germany in the 1960s and is fluent in the language); the little-known story of Thomas Mann's Brazilian mother, Júlia; and the three intersecting stories linking Freud, Mann, and Júlia. As in Teolinda's other works, the focus is on Júlia's inner life, her experiences being transplanted at a young age by her German-born father from Brazil to Germany after her mother's death, and her suffering at the hands of her strict Lutheran paternal relatives. The racism underlying her rejection by the family, the contrast of Júlia's inner world with that of her life in Germany, and the stark shifts between the dominant male voices and Julia's as she attempts to share memories of Brazil with her children present numerous opportunities to work with register, language shifts, narrative structure, and style. The book is an unusual story of migration, cultural contact, and the clash of the old world with the new. The underlying themes of domination and exploitation not just of countries but of women's minds and bodies invite a focus on exploring the potential of English to express alterity amid rigid hierarchies.

The End Is the Beginning —and Translation as Agency

In June 2023 Terry and I embarked on a trip to Iceland, Greenland, Newfoundland, and Nova Scotia. We were excited finally to explore this part of the northern hemisphere and to have the opportunity to cross the Arctic Circle. Iceland was a marvelous discovery, and I had spent months reading Icelandic fiction in my spare time, including its one Nobel Prize–winning novel, *Independent People* (1946), by Halldór Laxness, translated by J. A. Thompson. The translation is magnificent and captures the richness and subtlety of the original prose as well as the grandeur and mystery of Iceland's otherworldly landscape. I was awed at how Thompson rendered the passages of folk poetry, with full rhyme and rhythm, and incorporated the poetry into the dialogue marked by spontaneous verse recited among friends as a form of competition. The book brought Iceland to life in my imagination and colored my perception of the country on the ground. We spent three delightful days in Reykjavík exploring the city and environs of the island's southern "Golden Circle" and experiencing the prominent book culture at bookstore–coffee houses. I enjoyed learning about the Icelandic language almost as much as seeing the scenery. Only about 350,000 people speak it. The island, which is basically a basaltic rock, has provided a time capsule for the language that was known as Old Norse, the language of the Vikings. Given the island's 1,200-year history of isolation, Icelandic closely resembles Old Norse. It has common lineage with Norwegian, Swedish, Danish, and Faroese. The Icelanders take pride in claiming that one citizen in ten is a writer, and that was clear in every bookstore we visited. Translators of their literature are also held in high esteem.

When we embarked on our cruise ship, we experienced the first signs that the trip would be altered by the present danger of climate change. Our departure from the Reykjavík cruise terminal was delayed by a vicious windstorm, which prevented the ship from entering two scheduled southern ports. When we left Iceland after visiting northern ports, we were informed that the ship could not stop as scheduled in Greenland and Newfoundland because ice was blocking the harbor. This is a counterintuitive sign of climate change: ice melt from glaciers forms blocks of ice in the sea. It is a fact that Greenland is melting. Our next port of call, Halifax, Nova Scotia, was suffering the effects of the massive forest fires that were raging in eastern Canada and swept through the Halifax-area communities of Tantallon and Hammonds. The smoke from the fires followed us all the way to the New York harbor, where the usually magnificent entrance was veiled in a thick shroud of toxic smoke fumes. The view of the Statue of Liberty and Ellis Island was obscured. My eyes teared up not just from the smoke but from the thought of my grandparents, father, and aunt arriving at Ellis Island so many years ago. My grandfather, a forecaster and proponent of globalization, would not have predicted that climate change would be one of the unintended consequences that would endanger the planet in the lifetimes of his grandchildren and great-grandchildren, in whom he placed so much hope for the life of his family beyond Nazi Germany.

The state of the world and the environment calls for continued growth of the translation profession. As language workers, we can apply our knowledge and skills to solve pressing world problems involving social justice, the environment, preservation of civil rights and freedom of expression, peacekeeping, and the continuing enrichment of humanistic studies. In addition to gaining recognition for our work and having our names routinely placed on book covers, our lives as translators are worthy of recognition. Many translators are women, and we can draw attention to the role that gender plays in social perceptions. Our work is fundamental to the advance of knowledge and to the uplift of traditionally underrepresented voices. Translation is much more than rendering meaning. In the words of Meg Matich, translator of Auður Jónsdóttir's *Quake* (2022), "it somehow births something that has a past, and teaches this reborn creature how to tell its story in another language. And then teaches it again to tell it *well*" (288). The words "translated by" will no longer connote invisibility but active agency. Our art/craft invites us to draw on our life experiences, our aesthetic sensibilities, our sense of our role in society, our relationship with books and the authors we translate, and our relationship with our readers to build something new. There is room for many at the table, including those who translate from their native language into a second language, those of diverse backgrounds and ethnicities whose choice of texts and translation style informs us of stories different from our own, rising translators whose energy, idealism, and aspirations inspire us, and those of my generation who learned from our predecessors and opened pathways for those who have followed. I place my trust in the next generations of linguists, cross-cultural communications specialists, translators, and the readers of translations to carry on this good work, knowing that they can confidently dwell in possibility.

Acknowledgments

My thanks to Mario Pereira, executive editor of Tagus Press, for our many years of close collaboration and for encouraging me to write this book. My appreciation goes to Daniel Shapiro for his encouragement and support throughout my translating years, for inviting me to join the editorial board of *Review: Literature and Arts of the Americas*, and for the opportunity to guest edit three issues of the journal. I am grateful to my family for reading my manuscript and providing thoughtful suggestions and comments that jogged my memory on specific details of our shared lives through many cities and continents—and kept me honest! Thank you to my "two husbands," Jonathan Lowe and Terry McCoy, for standing by me on my life's journey and loving me for who I am, with my baggage of *weltfremd* and *Fernweh*. To my siblings, Peggy (Margaret Elaine) Jaret, Fred (Alfred Kenneth) Schlomann, and Rob (Robert Henry) Schlomann, often unruly sidekicks on our wild ride around the world, I extend my love and appreciation. Peggy has been my most faithful reader and companion on many travel adventures. Our penchant for triggering each other into sidesplitting laughter over life's absurd moments is a wonderful tonic. We deeply mourn the loss of our late brother, Rick (Frederick Ernest) Schlomann, who tragically died of colon cancer at the age of sixty-one. All our names were given in the Jewish tradition of naming children after close relatives: Peggy was named for our great-grandmother Helena Bromberg, who died in the extermination camp; Rob was named for her son Robert, who died with her; Fred is named for our *Opa* Alfred Schlomann, and Rick for a German uncle of my father's and for my father. Fred's and Rick's seemingly redundant names have given us many good laughs. I am the namesake of two American aunts, my mother's sisters: Anne Guthrie, my godmother (a Virginia poet who was a pianist and went to Julliard), and Beatrice Elizabeth Allen, who was a talented designer for Steuben glass in New York and attended theological seminary. I thank my children, Alicia Misarti and Alan Lowe, for surviving my frequent absences for work and travel and for making me so proud of their many accomplishments. Thank you to Julie McCoy D'Amico and Dan McCoy for adopting a stepmother who, I hope, hasn't seemed too wicked! To my "hermanas," sister translators errant—Suzanne Jill Levine, Kate Hedeen, D. P. Snyder, Allison Markin Powell, Kelsi Venada, Bruna Dantas Lobato, Annelise Finegan, Jenny McPhee, Andréia Guerini, and others too numerous to mention—you have my solidarity and affection. I thank my students for motivating me to keep working and for teaching me by helping me see the world through their eyes. And not least, my love and gratitude go out to all my grandchildren: Sarah, Amanda, Kellie, Nicole, Tedi, and Julian. You give me hope for the future.

References

Agee, Philip. 1975. *Inside the Company: CIA Diary.* New York: Stonehill.

Alter, Alexandra. 2022. "An Urgent Mission for Literary Translators: Bringing Ukrainian Voices to the West." *New York Times*, March 10. https://www.nytimes.com/2022/03/10/books/ukraine-translate-books.html.

Astor, Michael. 2020. "Rubem Fonseca, Giant of Brazilian Literature, Dies at 94." *New York Times*, April 20.

Barnstone, Willis. 2017. "The Bloody History of Bible Translators." *Los Angeles Review of Books*, November 11.

BBC News. 2015. "Bolivia: Group Translates Facebook into Native Language." *News from Elsewhere*, 17 September. https://www.bbc.com/news/blogs-news-from-elsewhere-34279302.

Becker, Eric M. B. 2016. Introduction to *Írisz: The Orchids* by Noemi Jaffe. *Electric Lit* 214. https://electricliterature.com/irisz-the-orchids-noemi-jaffe/.

Bishop, Elizabeth. 1965. *Questions of Travel.* New York: Farrar, Straus and Giroux.

Bishop, Elizabeth. 1983. *Elizabeth Bishop: The Complete Poems 1927-1979*. New York: Farrar, Straus and Giroux.

Book Center Brazil. 2022. "Clarice Lispector: Author and Translator." Book Center Brazil, January 18. https://centrointernacionaldolivro.wordpress.com/2022/01/18/clarice-lispector-author-and-translator/.

Borges, Jorge Luis. 2007. *Labyrinths*. Translated by Donald Yates and James Irby. New York: New Directions.

Bosi, Alfredo, ed. 1973. *Os Sertões by Euclides da Cunha*. Didactic edition. São Paulo: Editora Cultrix.

Braga Pinto, César A. 1993. "An Other of One's Own: Clarice Lispector, Hélène Cixous, and American Audiences." Master's thesis, San Francisco State University, May.

Breen, Amanda. 2020. "This Is Who We Are: Susan Bernofsky." Columbia University School of the Arts News Archive, December 14. https://arts.columbia.edu/news/who-we-are-susan-bernofsky.

Briggs, Kate. 2017. *This Little Art*. London: Fitzcarraldo Editions.

Cheuse, Alan. 1983. "The 'Disappeared' and the Jettisoned." *New York Times Book Review*, July 24, 10.

Cuenca, J. P. 2021. "Nothing's Older than the Recent Past." Translated by Ezra E. Fitz. *Review: Literature and Arts of the Americas* 54, no. 1: 17–23.

da Cunha, Euclides. 1944. *Rebellion in the Backlands*. Translated by Samuel A. Putnam. Chicago: University of Chicago Press.

———. 2010. *Backlands: The Canudos Campaign*. Translated and with a preface by Elizabeth Lowe. New York: Penguin.

Davis, Lydia. 2021. "Twenty-One Pleasures of Translating (and a Silver Lining)." In *Essays Two*. New York: Farrar, Straus & Giroux.

de Queirós, Eça. 2015. *Saint Christopher*. Translated by Gregory Rabassa and Earl Fitz. Dartmouth, MA: Tagus Press.

Desikachar, T. K. V. 1995. "The Yoga Sutra of Patanjali." In *The Heart of Yoga*, 145–215. Rochester, VT: Inner Traditions International.

Fitts, Dudley. 1965. "Brazilians All." *New York Times Book Review*, August 8, 4.

Fitz, Earl. 2018. "Translating with Greg Rabassa: The Last Book." *Exchanges*, April 18.

Franco, Jean. 1966. Review of *Esau and Jacob* by Joaquim Maria Machado de Assis. *Times Literary Supplement*, February 17, 1966, 122.

Gentzler, Edwin. 2001. *Contemporary Translation Theories*. Toronto: Multilingual Matters.

Goldfajn, Tal. 2020. "'The Greatest Defect of This Book Is You, Reader': On Two Translations of Machado de Assis's 'The Posthumous Memoirs of Brás Cubas.'" *Los Angeles Review of Books*, September 22.

Hallett, Elisabeth. 2003. "Rio." In *Still Mystified: The Poems in My Life*. N.p.: iUniverse.

Hedeen, Katherine M. 2019. "Manifesto?" *Asymptote*, April. https://www.asymptotejournal.com/special-feature/katherine-hedeen-manifesto/.

Helgason, Hallgrímur. 2018. *Woman at 1,000 Degrees*. Translated by Brian FitzGibbon. Chapel Hill, NC: Algonquin Books.

Hond, Paul. 2021–22. "The Peculiar Perils of Literary Translation." *Columbia Magazine*, Winter. https://magazine.columbia.edu/article/peculiar-perils-literary-translation.

Jackson, K. David, ed. 2006. *Oxford Anthology of the Brazilian Short Story*. Oxford: Oxford University Press.

Jaffe, Noemi. 2016. *What Are the Blind Men Dreaming*. Translated by Julia Sanches and Ellen Elias Bursać. Dallas: Deep Vellum.

Jónsdóttir, Auður. 2022. *Quake*. Translated by Meg Matich. New York: Dottir Press.

Lahiri, Jhumpa. 2023. *Translating Myself and Others*. Princeton, NJ: Princeton University Press.

Levine, Suzanne Jill. 2009. *The Subversive Scribe*. Champaign, IL: Dalkey Archive Press.

Lispector, Clarice. 1949. *A cidade sitiada*. Rio de Janeiro: Editora a Noite.

———. 1988. *The Passion According to G. H.* Translated by Ronald W. Sousa. Minneapolis: University of Minnesota Press.

———. 1989. *The Stream of Life*. Translated by Elizabeth Lowe and Earl Fitz. Minneapolis: University of Minnesota Press.

Lobo Antunes, António. 2019. *Until Stones Become Lighter than Water.* Translated by Jeff Love. New Haven, CT: Yale University Press.

Lowe, Elizabeth. 1979. "The Passion According to C. L.: Elizabeth Lowe Interviews Clarice Lispector." *Review* 24:34–37.

———. 2012. "'*E o sertão é um paraíso . . .*' : The Case for Re-translating *Os Sertões*." *Translation Review* 80, no. 1: 1–12. https://www.tandfonline.com/doi/abs/10.1080/07374836.2010.10524026.

———. 2023. "Nélida Piñon: Brazil's Scheherazade." *Review* 107: 257-260.

Lowe, Elizabeth, and Earl E. Fitz. 2007. *Translation and the Rise of Inter-American Literature.* Gainesville: University Press of Florida.

Machado de Assis, Joachim. 2000. *Esau and Jacob*. Translated by Elizabeth Lowe. Oxford: Oxford University Press.

Mason, Wyatt. 2017. "The First Woman to Translate the 'Odyssey' into English." *New York Times Magazine*, November 2. https://www.nytimes.com/2017/11/02/magazine/the-first-woman-to-translate-the-odyssey-into-english.html.

Max, D. T. 2023. "The Novelist Whose Inventions Went Too Far." *New Yorker*, March 13.

McPhee, Jenny. 2000. Review of *Esau and Jacob* by Joaquim Maria Machado de Assis. *New York Times Book Review*, November 26.

Mead, Robert. 1978. "After the Boom: The Fate of Latin American Literature in English Translation." *Américas* 30, no. 4: 2–8.

Monteiro, Pedro Meira. 2010. "Todo instante: A ficção de João Almino." *Luso-Brazilian Review* 47, no. 1: 61–70.

Monteiro Batista, Adelaide. 1993. *João de Melo e a literatura açoriana*. Lisbon: Publicações Dom Quixote.

Moser, Benjamin. 2009. *Why This World: A Biography of Clarice Lispector*. Oxford: Oxford University Press.

———. 2023. "A Lost Interview with Clarice Lispector." *New Yorker*, February 13.

PEN America. 2023. *The 2023 Manifesto on Literary Translation*. April. https://pen.org/report/translation-manifesto/.

Pereira, Gilberto G. 2023. "Um tributo a Nélida Piñon, nossa Scherezade." *Ermira*, January 8. https://ermiracultura.com.br/2023/01/08/um-tributo-a-nelida-pinon-nossa-scherezade/.

Polizzotti, Mark. 2018. *Sympathy for the Traitor: A Translation Manifesto.* Cambridge, MA: MIT Press.

Rabassa, Gregory. 1989. "No Two Snowflakes Are Alike: Translation as Metaphor." In *The Craft of Translation*, edited by John Biguenet and Rainer Schulte, 1–12. Chicago: University of Chicago Press.

———. 2005. *If This Be Treason: Translation and Its Dyscontents*. New York: New Directions.

Rundle, Christopher. 2018. "Translation and Fascism." In *The Routledge Handbook of Translation and Politics*, edited by Fruela Fernández and Jonathan Evans, 29–47. New York: Taylor & Francis.

Santana, Jose Carlos Barreto de. 2005. "Natural Science and Brazilian Nationality: *Os Sertões* by Euclides da Cunha." *Science in Context* 18:225–37.

Schlomann, Alfred F. 1940. "Measuring Management in Business Enterprises: The Laws Governing Business Enterprises." Unpublished manuscript.

Schwartz, Lloyd. 1991. "Elizabeth Bishop and Brazil." *New Yorker*, September 30.

Schulte, Rainer, and John Biguenet. 1989. Introduction to *The Craft of Translation*, edited by John Biguenet and Rainer Schulte. Chicago: University of Chicago Press.

Shahmirzadi, Atefeh Akbari. 2019. "Introduction to One Hundred Years of Solitude." https://www.docsity.com/en/introduction-to-one-hundred-years-of-solitude/8917010/.

Silva-Reis, Dennys. 2019. "Black Feminist Thought and Translation Studies: Interview with Patrícia Hill Collins." *Revista Ártemis* 27, no. 1: 222–28.

Stavans, Ilan. 2010. Introduction to Euclides da Cunha, *Backlands: The Canudos Campaign*. Translated by Elizabeth Lowe. New York: Penguin.

Straile, Paula D., and Earl E. Fitz. 1995. "*Rebellion in the Backlands*, by Samuel Putnam, and *Os Sertões*, by Euclides da Cunha: A Comparative Translation Study." *Translation Review* 47:45–51.

Szulc, Tad. 1960. "Northeast Brazil Poverty Breeds a Threat of Revolt." *New York Times*, October 31.

Thurman, Judith. 2023. "Mother Tongue." *New Yorker*, September 11.

Valente, Paulo Gurgel. 2021. "At Home with Clarice." Clarice Lispector, November 11. https://site.claricelispector.ims.com.br/en/2021/11/11/at-home-with-clarice/.

Venuti, Lawrence, ed. 1992. *Rethinking Translation: Discourse, Subjectivity, Ideology*. London: Routledge.

Wechsler, Robert. 1998. *Performing Without a Stage: The Art of Literary Translation*. North Haven, CT: Catbird Press.

Wei, Xuehu, et al. 2023. "Native Language Differences in the Structural Connectome of the Human Brain." *NeuroImage* 270 (April 15).

Wüster, Eugen. 2004. "The Structure of the Linguistic World of Concepts and Its Representation in Dictionaries." *Terminology* 10, no. 2: 281–306.

Elizabeth Lowe

Photo by Adrienne Fletcher

Born in New York City, and whose academic career began in the early 1970s at The City University of New York, Elizabeth Lowe translated over thirty works by Lusophone writers from Brazil, Portugal, and Africa. She was one of the first to translate Jorge Amado, Clarice Lispector, Rubem Fonseca, Nélida Pinõn, and António Lobo Antunes. She is the author of *The City in Brazilian Literature* (1982), and co-author with Earl E. Fitz of *Translation and the Rise of Inter-American Literature* (2008), along with many scholarly articles and book chapters. She has held professorial roles at several institutions, where she has contributed to developing translation studies programs, most recently at University of Illinois Champaign-Urbana and New York University. She served as FLAD Endowed Chair of Portuguese Studies at UMass Dartmouth in Spring 2022. Her honors include an NEA Literary Translation Fellowship, a National Endowment for the Humanities grant, National Science Foundation grants for research on language preservation, Fulbright fellowships to Colombia and Brazil, and recognition by the Brazilian Academy of Letters. Her memoir, "Translating from the Portuguese: A Life Translated," has been featured in *Review Magazine* (CUNY).